Beluga: a farewell to whales

BELUGA

a farewell to whales

PIERRE BÉLAND

Lyons & Burford, Publishers

Printed in the United States of America

10 9 8 7 6 5 4 3 2 1

Design by LaBreacht Design

Library of Congress Cataloging-in-Publication Data
Béland, Pierre, 1947–
        Beluga : a farewell to whales / Pierre Béland
        p.   cm.
        ISBN 1-55821-398-8 (cloth)
        1. White whale. 2. White whale—Saint Lawrence River Region.
I. Title.
QL737.C433B428   1996
599.5'3—dc20   96-2661
                                                           CIP

CONTENTS

To Andrée Boulanger, who had many dreams.
Those she did not live,
she passed on to her children.

ACKNOWLEDGMENTS

The colleagues with whom I have worked closely on the beluga in the St. Lawrence have been my true inspiration. You will meet several in the pages that follow, and much of what I know has been learned through them. What has been achieved has resulted from the challenges we set for each other and from our common striving to learn, which turned into a dedication to preserve, as the grisly truth emerged. They, as much as the whales, have become friends. We have collaborated with a much larger group of scientists, and those whose names do not appear herein are not forgotten. We are collectively indebted to the many institutions that have supported our research through so many years.

I am also grateful to those in the science, regulation, and business sectors who have relentlessly opposed my views over the years: they have forced me to search ever beyond. Many people have provided me with factual information and/or corrected earlier versions of the manuscript, including Michel Fournier, Lou Garibaldi, Fred Hotson, Laura Ludwig, Ken Norris, Randall Reeves, Pierre Richard, Peter Scheifele, Richard Sears, and Roland Tremblay. I am especially indebted to François Roy, who researched various historical facts. The characters and events in this book are true, although I have had to imagine the motivations of the nonliving and of those whom I have never met. The stories are meant to be exact, but any error of fact is mine. The original stimulus that launched this book came from Greg Shaw, from my editor Lilly Golden, both of whom trusted that I was a writer, and from my wife Marie, who believes I can be anything I want to be.

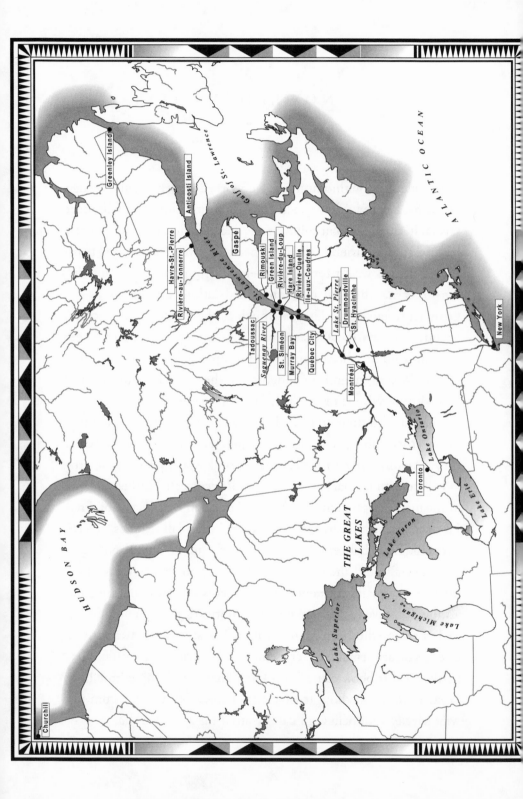

PREFACE

Since time immemorial, there have been beluga whales in the estuary of the St. Lawrence River in eastern North America. Their fossil skeletons are buried in the sediments of an ancient sea that formed and vanished in the wake of the last glaciation ten thousand years ago. Their teeth and bones are among the archaeological remains found at Amerindian hunting sites that have been dated at around A.D. 200. This white whale entered the written history of North America when French navigators came to explore the St. Lawrence river in the sixteenth century. Within a hundred years, and into the first half of this century, colonists who settled the shore were killing the whales each year by the hundreds for their hides and their oil. Between the two great world wars, belugas were also slaughtered because they were perceived as threats to the cod and salmon fisheries.

After the Second World War, the demand for, or the availability of, beluga products in the St. Lawrence declined sharply, and fisheries authorities lost interest in the animal for the next thirty-five years. In 1979, after concern over the belugas' reduced numbers had been raised, the population was afforded legal protection by the Canadian government. In the meantime, however, more insidious but no less effective threats had arisen in the wake of industrialization and intensive agriculture. Habitat degradation and a variety of man-made toxic chemicals introduced into the Great Lakes and St. Lawrence basins have replaced the dangers of prior centuries. Of the thousands of beluga whales that roamed the river, the estuary, and the Gulf of St. Lawrence at the turn of the century, only a few hundred remain. And those that are found dead each year, adrift or on shore, show the effects of long-term exposure to toxic chemicals.

This book relates the story of the white whale in the St. Lawrence. It also tells the story of the river and of the people who lived on its shores, both of which had some bearing on the destiny of the whales. Humans, the river, and the whales come together in the true tales I will tell. Most of these stories are about my own experience while I studied the St. Lawrence and its beluga whale. For this animal has become intricately woven into my own life ever since I first touched a stranded carcass on a beach on a September afternoon years ago. In retrospect, it seems that all I have done since then is to try to understand what has happened to the river of my childhood, and what the fate of its belugas means to me and to my fellow human beings.

Pierre Béland
Spring 1996

Book of the Dead

*L*ining up my car on the pier at Rivière-du-Loup on the south shore of the St. Lawrence, I realize how much I love to board a ferry. Particularly this one, with its childhood memories of a large white ship cruising away on the river. As a young boy wading at low tide among the seaweed-covered rocks, I was halted in my search for clam worms by the sight of the ferryboat. I would watch it become a tiny craft before it disappeared in midstream behind the long green streak of Hare Island which hides the coastline on the other side. I had never been on the water, never been on the ship, never seen its berth across the river. I could only imagine that the boat would take its passengers for a tour around the island and find an idyllic beach on which to land everyone for a picnic, as families did in one of my picture books.

I am on standby in my old green Volvo, enjoying the bustle that surrounds a docking ship. The Sunday fishermen move over with their lines dangling to make room for the landing. The leads to the mooring cables explode from the ship like broken coil springs, startling the gulls that are always hawking for some scrap of food. The drivers about to disembark are anxious, their car engines running, their heads perked up behind steering wheels, as if they might be able to leave before the boat even docks. On the pier, in the meantime, the drivers waiting on the dock look equally worried, contemplating how they will squeeze down the steep ramp into the ship, which sits so low on the tidal estuary.

My car is the last to board behind a huge trailer truck that rattles the openwork steel ramp. The ship sinks noticeably and rises up again after the truck is finally aboard, leaving me temporarily halted at a steep angle. When signaled to move forward, I show my free pass to Officer Belley. I know him well, and as usual he invites me to the wheelhouse for the crossing. Driving into the bowels of the ship, I get a last glimpse of the fishermen holding onto their rods on the wharf. They stare at each passenger entering the ship as if they were double agents entrusted with the compiling of statistics on the profitability of the ferry. They count me, too, at each sailing, but they don't seem to remember that I was one of them many years ago.

What brings me here nowadays is not the fish lurking under the greenish brown surface but the bigger animals who feed on them. Mammals like us, blind in murky waters, but possessing their own efficient means of catching fish. Porpoises, we called them when I was a kid on the wharf, still unaware of their true identity. Like us, the whales would move back to their favorite spot to resume fishing as soon as the ferry left. The boat's propeller would stir the mud, bringing food up through the water column for fish to feed on. And for mammals to catch the fish. Kids and whales. From my favorite fishing spot on the wharf, a clam worm wiggling on the hook at the end of my line, I watched the whales' gleaming crescents on the water, and heard their blows mixing with our laughter. I often wondered if they could make out against the sky our dark silhouettes and dazzling haloes. I wondered if they could hear our calls every time we caught a fish.

I park on the car deck among the other sardines, who can barely open their cans to get out. Most are families on vacation, the children excited to be on a real ship at sea, their parents somewhat anxious to get to the other side. Presently, they seem unable to make up their minds about whether to take a sweater and other things along, stressed as they are by the sign that reads DO NOT STAY IN CAR FOR THE CROSSING. I wait until the main herd has reached the upper deck, then climb up and try to find a nice hidden spot where I can scan the river in peace. I am eager to see if there are whales in the vicinity, and my search for them must be a private affair: I may see an animal that I know by name when the other passengers would see only one more beluga whale.

A few minutes after the ship has left the dock, a small group of whales surfaces in the distance, heading upstream on the tide along Hare Island. No one else has seen them, for all that is noticeable are flashes of sunlight that come and go in the distance. I know that such sparkles on a windless day can only be whales. Some time later, we get closer to the whales, and a number of passengers spot them. Some kids who may have heard about them on TV call out excitedly, pulling at the sleeves of their parents, who, unable to make out anything, say there cannot be whales so close to land. Still others, with the look of people who are getting what they paid for, respond contentedly that this is what the travel guidebook said. And then there are those who watch in silence and with respect, conscious of witnessing animals in their own environment, doing their job honestly, and deserving not to be disturbed.

The belugas roll smoothly with an unhurried determination, as always instilling in me a measure of serenity. Unlike the slender dolphins, they do not speed or jump as they come out for air. They look more like small, plump whales than porpoises. They do not swim close to each other yet move together as a single pod of adults, whiter than the surf on a wave in the wind, opaque as creamy milk. They are so bright against the dark water that you would swear you could see them miles away, even beyond the curvature of the earth. At close range, their bodies show no color patterns, bands, or streaks, although they usually bear scratches of undetermined origin. One animal has nicks across the barely noticeable ridge that runs along the middle of its back, where the dorsal fin stands in other species. The lack of a fin makes it difficult for the untrained eye to follow the progression of a beluga's body when it arches over the surface of the water. From a distance, the animal seems to emerge and sink without moving ahead, as if a crescent of the moon had been pushed up from underwater for exactly three seconds and pulled back in.

I do not recognize a known animal but notice a young boy and girl looking at me intently. Feeling discovered, I climb to the officers' quarters on the top deck. As soon as I walk into the wheelhouse, careful not to trip over the high sill, Captain Harvey asks me about the whales: *How is your work going this year?* But I have my own questions for the crew. Have they seen many young this season? The exchange of data on the whales is our greeting ritual. I give some details about our latest findings while perusing the wheelhouse, always amazed at how spotless and well ordered it is. I am careful not to let my fingers touch the polished brass lining the windows and the navigation instruments.

I pick up a pair of binoculars to look at the river toward the southwest, where we are headed.

The ferry makes six crossings a day from April to the end of the Christmas holidays, each time spending an hour and a half in the heart of the beluga range in the St. Lawrence. Technically, the domain of the whales is an estuary—an area where fresh water from a river mixes with saltwater from the sea. The map, however, labels this body of water the St. Lawrence "River," and that is what people here usually call it. But unlike a river, the St. Lawrence flows downstream only half the time, its main current reversed every six hours by the tide. Twice a day, millions of tons of light brown water are flushed downstream, exposing the outer fringe of the riverbed. Sailboats that enter the marina at Rivière-du-Loup at high tide will be sitting in the mud as much as eighteen feet lower six hours later. Then, in one slow breath, green saltwaters flood the shore again, bringing in seaweed, marine fish, and seabirds, along with assorted seals and whales. Gazing upstream or downstream, your eyes can see only water as far as the horizon. It sparkles, it is cold, and it has drowned many ships and killed even more mariners. That is why those who live by the lower St. Lawrence also call it the sea.

At Rivière-du-Loup, the St. Lawrence is twelve miles wide; across it are mountains, at the foot of which the water is four hundred feet deep. The St. Lawrence boasts a fjord, which lurks under the fog to the northeast like the fjords on the coast of Norway in the North Atlantic. Ancient saline waters reside permanently in these troughs, reminders of when the St. Lawrence truly was an arm of the sea and the beluga, an arctic species, came into this area. Around twenty thousand years ago, much of Canada and the northern United States was covered in glaciers, and arctic whales and seals fed at the ice edge in the Atlantic off the exposed continental shelf. Then, as the climate started to warm up, the Laurentian ice sheet melted away and the sea level rose over the continent, which had sunk considerably under the immense weight of ice. In the northeast, marine waters penetrated into and beyond the Gulf of St. Lawrence, filling a huge area west almost to the Great Lakes and southwest to New York and Vermont. Finback, humpback, and bowhead whales; narwhals and harbor porpoises; harp, bearded, and hooded seals came into this inland sea. Belugas roamed in huge herds, and their skeletons account for most of the whale remains found in the sediments deposited at the bottom of this Champlain Sea 9,300 to 12,400 years ago. In ecological terms, this was the arctic of the day.

In time, relieved from its burden of ice, the land rose, the basin dried up, and the St. Lawrence River took form in its midst. Its lower course, where the Rivière-du-Loup ferry now crosses, remains an ever-changing realm between the continent and the ocean. It is in this estuary, that the North Atlantic, hundreds of miles away to the east, and the Great Lakes, hundreds of miles inland, meet every day. As freshwater rushes out to sea at the surface, a cold wedge of saline water flows inward beneath it, all the way from the Gulf of St. Lawrence and the ocean. This frigid layer, replenished by cooling during the harsh winter, surges to the surface where submarine walls of rock stop its course, or when the wind blows from the land. Here, although the climate warmed up long ago and narwhals, bowhead whales, and walrus have departed, belugas have remained, along with a few arctic fish and crustaceans that thrive in this arctic oasis far from the polar region.

It does not look like an oasis at all in winter. By Christmas, the river is already covered in pack ice. Floes drift from shore to shore, up and down the river, slaves to wind and tide, and pile up in huge stacks all along the coast and around the rim of every island. When the wind is from the northwest and masses of frozen arctic air swoop down the mountains, the deep water in the troughs at their foot surges to the surface, where it smokes like a smoldering fire. This weather signals the season of the harp seals, who come in to breed on the floes and to feed on capelin made sluggish by the freezing water. For a few weeks, the seals take over the estuary. The beluga have deserted it for the gulf, where they share open waters with the hardiest of sea ducks. By then, the ferry has stopped running until the spring to avoid being crushed by floes in the middle of the night.

⌒⟶

I am happy to chat with the crew, who have become dear to me over the years, but I have something else in mind. I want to know if the watch officer has spotted the whales that I saw minutes ago from my restricted view on the deck below. Pretending to amble around and somewhat ashamed of my deviousness, I walk to the chart table. On it, next to the ship's logbook, lies another book, the whale logbook. It is a binder that I have prepared for the crew, with hundreds of identical pages, each one a reduced photocopy of the nautical chart showing the ship's course between the shores and around the tip of Hare Island. One page per crossing, on which the officers have agreed to mark down their whale sightings. The book is opened at today's crossing. There they are: six whales going upstream by the island, five minutes ago.

From March to December, the whale logbook is where live beluga sightings are recorded every day. The voluntary work of the crew is important because the ferryboat's route is inhabited by a large number of females with young. What happens here is critical to the future of the St. Lawrence beluga whale population. Several more seasons of dedicated work will be required before any pattern in the whales' movements can be recognized and any change in their numbers detected. Every day, the crew is on the lookout, hoping to make more entries in their book than they did the previous year.

My own book is much smaller, and I would rather not add anything to it. It is a record of dead beluga whales, with 180 entries since the fall of 1982. The St. Lawrence belugas are a small resident population of about five hundred animals, isolated from other belugas, who live in the Arctic. Fifteen dead animals per year is therefore a sizeable statistic—and I may be recording only a fraction of the deaths, certainly few of those that occur during winter. Beluga whales can live thirty years and more, but healthy females in their prime give birth to a single calf only once every three years. This means that replacement is slow under the best of conditions. Even slight disturbances can check the growth of a small population. The present St. Lawrence belugas are the remnant of a population of several thousands who were heavily exploited for almost three hundred years. When they were given legal protection in 1979, only about five hundred whales remained. Since then, the population has failed to recover. My Book of the Dead tells why: the whales are dying of pollution.

Even as I write it, I realize how strong this last statement is— "Far too strong for a scientist," many of my colleagues would say. I would not have dared say such a thing a few years ago. Maybe I have grown bolder as my experience and interest in these animals have matured. But in fact I am simply echoing the conclusion that most observers of our work have come to. It is very plain.

By the time a St. Lawrence beluga whale reaches age sixteen, its body's burden of mercury has already exceeded the load considered to be necessary to cause developmental and neurological effects in humans. This load increases as long as the whale lives in that river, which means until its death. Take organohalogens, for another example. These are a family of man-made chemicals that includes insecticides like DDT, dieldrin, and mirex, as well as industrial chemicals like polychlorobiphenyls (PCBs). Because of the hazardous nature of these compounds, ships on the St. Lawrence carrying waste with more than fifty milligrams of PCBs per kilogram (or fifty parts per million) require a special transit permit. An average male beluga roaming these same waters already has that concentration of PCBs in his blubber by age nine—without the permit—and that level will double by the time he is twenty-two. Adult females are more fortunate: their blubber PCB levels will not reach fifty ppm before age thirty-four—an age very few belugas ever reach. But the lower level in females is not actually a good sign. It is only by unloading their contaminants onto their calves through nursing that females reduce their level of intoxication.

↩

The ferry is now coasting close to Hare Island, that imagined haven of my childhood. I scan its shore to locate the site where I finally landed recently on my first visit to the island. Even after all these years, the place still held an aura of mystery when I first approached it in a small research boat with two colleagues. It looked like a beautiful, unspoiled garden and would have been romantic, had I gone there for a picnic and not to answer a call about a dead beluga whale. We spent some time searching for the whale among the driftwood, dead reeds, and assorted plastic refuse littering the pebbles at the edge of the forest. After much effort, we found a tiny carcass. It was a newborn calf, and already several like him had been recorded in my Book of the Dead. They had died of intoxication or because their mothers had passed away, unable to survive the stress of giving birth.

The other pages in my book are mostly records of adults who suffered the effects of long-term exposure to chemicals, as opposed to acute poisoning. There have been no mass mortalities in the St. Lawrence, only unspectacular deaths of single individuals drifting to the shore, as if the population were undergoing slow attrition. We would not even know about the belugas' plight if we had not taken these carcasses every year to the necropsy room at the veterinary school of the University of Montréal, far upriver, driving for hours through the night on the highway, hauling strange horizontal ghosts like gigantic alien sausages.

It all started in September 1982, when a veterinarian from Agriculture Canada dropped into my laboratory on the university campus in Rimouski. He told me about his summer sailing trips on the St. Lawrence and in Saguenay fjord, where he had often observed white whales come to investigate his boat. He thought that studying these animals would be a welcome change from his regular and tiring travels all across the Gaspé Peninsula, treating cows and sheep. He wondered whether the federal government research center that I was heading at the time had an interest in the whales. I had to tell him that we were a fisheries ecology research center, already involved in several research projects, none of which had anything to do with belugas. In retrospect, I may have even added that whales ate fish and that our job was to understand how fish were being produced in the river, not how they were being consumed. Over the next few weeks, this gentleman came to see me a few more times, always enquiring about beluga whales and invariably leaving his name and phone number. I came to find his visits rather annoying. I have long since forgotten his phone number, but I remember his name very well: Daniel Martineau.

Soon afterward, Dr. David Sergeant, who had been researching belugas in the Arctic and the St. Lawrence, was invited on campus to give a talk on his work. I phoned Dr. Martineau, happy at last to have something to offer him. On the appointed day, we were holed up with other members of academia in a university classroom, both listening to David's talk. He was about halfway through his slides when my secretary peeked into the room and silently handed me a note: a dead beluga had just been found washed on shore a few kilometers away. It was the first such notice we had ever received, and it was undoubtedly due to the presence of Dr. Sergeant among us. As soon as the talk was over, Daniel and I rushed up to David with the note, and within minutes, all three of us were driving toward the lighthouse at Pointe-au-Père, where I saw my very first beluga whale in its entirety.

I had had some exposure to belugas when I was a child drifting through the summer holidays at a small village by the name of Rivière-Ouelle. Sometimes I went for walks with my mother on the beach along the St. Lawrence when she managed to slip away from her household chores. We waded over the flat at low tide in the small haze that rose from the cold mud exposed to the sun, and I stopped here and there to overturn a stone with a stick, careful not to let my shoes dangling from my hands fall in the soft mud. I remember vividly how my mother would call to me, excitedly pointing at some inconspicuous specks out there on the majestic river. *Do you see them? Do you see them?* I would turn toward her instead of to the river, my feet sinking into the dark brown goo that left gray patches where it had dried on my calves.

My mother had always looked at the world the way she did on her first Christmas morning: everything to her was magic, beautiful, new. Her love for the river and for everything that lived in or by it burst out each time she walked on its shore. I had become blasé about her constant wonderments, but being a respectful child, I would take a look at the oceanlike expanse of water. Sometimes I saw the small white crescents on the water in the distance—not so different from the countless whitecaps borne in the wind that seemed to inhabit that moving kingdom perpetually. More often than not, I was not sure that I saw anything in particular. Those white flashes could just as well have been pieces of ice that had survived through the spring and that accounted for the water's being so cold all the time. *Yes, I see them,* I would answer, feeling uneasy about lying. *They are migrating upstream today,* my mother would say. *How numerous they are! Like waves on the sea! Look at those white whales! Look at those belugas!* I would look at her, thinking of the innumerable everyday things that she kept pointing out to me, whales being only one of them.

I eventually got to know these animals better, since they seemed to feed on the same fish that I tried to catch from the pier. But even then, I was never quite convinced that these white porpoises in the brownish water by the wharf were real whales. After all, the St. Lawrence was but a river, and all I ever saw were rounded white shapes without heads or tails. Now, a quarter of a century later, I stood on the beach next to a real beluga whale. I did not have to lie anymore: here it was, dead at my feet, rather smallish for a whale, stark white against the collage of blue mussel shells and brown seaweed on which it had so obtrusively landed. Having spent my childhood thinking that whales did not belong in the waters of a river, I now surmised that they belonged even less on its shore.

Daniel was immediately all around the body, measuring it, examining it, and discussing it with David. It looked very fresh and so perfectly smooth, with only a few rough patches inlaid with gravel where gulls had picked at the skin as the corpse drifted toward the shore. When I approached for a closer inspection, Daniel uttered fateful words: *Let's have a look inside.* I was flabbergasted. How does one look inside a whale? *Let's open it,* repeated Daniel. And with these words, he launched us on one of the most successful and challenging research projects any of us had ever been involved in. In the dozen years since that fateful day, we have examined scores of beluga carcasses along that same river. The shores of the St. Lawrence are dotted with sites that we have trodden to pick up dead whales. Strangely, every new death is still a wonder to me. Like my mother, I cannot get used to this everyday thing of life.

It was ironic that Daniel's interest in the whales, sparked by his observations of live animals in the river, had taken him away from his sailboat and back on the road and around the estuary and along the gulf shores, this time looking for dead animals. It was a very demanding project, and each new season saw him with a different helper, usually a summer student. Eventually, I took over the beachcombing part of the study and enlisted Richard Plante to help me. Fresh out of school, Richard had trained to become a fisherman but had discovered that he preferred to make fishing nets. My lab had commissioned him to make plankton nets and other gear for collecting various sea animals for scientific studies. One day, he walked in with a custom-made net for loading the dead bodies of marine mammals into our truck. Richard had tremendous energy and dedication. Together, we have retrieved dozens of carcasses of several species of whales and seals from the shores of the St. Lawrence.

It was exhilarating. At a single phone call we were off in a minute for a long trip. We spent many hours of hard work on the beach in all kinds of weather, which left us with the satisfaction of a physically demanding job well done. We savored the camaraderie and the splendor of daybreak on the water, when all was silent and we were on the road with a whale. But there was also sorrow. Driving along the sparsely inhabited shore, where long, dark stretches were broken by small villages with high-steepled churches, old trees alongside ancestral houses, and small wooden boats pulled up on shore, I passed through the country of my childhood. This was the land where I had been raised and where I had only dreamed of being able to visit every bay and cove. The dream had come true, except that I had become not an explorer but some kind of mortician.

Every call had to be answered. For some reason, the whales tended to die before sunrise or on weekends when I had some family outing. In the evening one December 31st, the phone rang at home and I could hardly understand the voice on the other end over the noise of the party going on at my place. I gathered that the speaker had been climbing some ice falls by the river in the morning and he had seen a white, rounded shape sticking out of the ice on the beach. He thought it might be a beluga. I told Richard and another friend, Paul Robichaud, who were among the crowd dancing and drinking to celebrate the end of another year. The following morning, the three of us set out walking on the shelf ice by the river, dragging our gear and my daughter Martine, who was seven years old. It was New Year's Day, thirty degrees below. The wind was a bitter northwester, the snow hard as wood, the ice like steel. We walked a mile and a half over the beach to the ice falls. The whale was there, creamy white, just a patch of its flank emerging from the snow and ice. We whacked at its ice casing with axes like miners in a quarry, until Martine went nearly numb with cold and we realized that all of us might die there too.

After finding my first dead whale in 1982, I could not help but think of its kin still out there in the river. Driving the long road from Rimouski to Montréal on business trips, I wondered where the whales were at that moment. I began taking the ferry to see what the whales did in June and July. But the season on the river is shorter for humans than for whales and by September the yachts and sailboats have been pulled up on shore. After the fishing nets have been retrieved and piled up in their sheds, after the navigation buoys have been taken out of the river and even the ferry has stopped passing the icebound island, where do the belugas roam? I spent hours scanning the river from a number of vantage points where I made regular stops.

I seldom saw belugas from the shore. There were none of the herds that my mother had once pointed out to me. The whales seemed to have stopped migrating upstream lately. Or downstream. I was afraid that they had begun to migrate into history. But I could not get a proper idea of what was happening at sea. Therefore in addition to our work on dead whales, we launched a series of projects to look at live whales and to understand how they lived. We ran surveys from the air and by boat, and were able to determine how many belugas there were and where they were. We photo-identified many animals and learned something about their social structure and movements. In particular, we discovered that females arrived at the area plied by the ferry in April, stayed through summer to give birth and to feed their young, and then left in October. We found out that there did not seem to be as many young belugas in this population as in those that lived farther north.

⤶

*T*he tide is ebbing now, and the brackish water from upstream bulges higher against the bow of the ferry. It is greenish brown and opaque, uninviting—aspects that are usually and wrongly associated with pollution. The water is rich with plankton and particles of organic matter that scatter sunlight, not with silt contaminated with the toxic chemicals found in the whales. The poisons are concealed within larger packages, mostly in fish, especially some species that migrate from far away. I arrived at this conclusion after adding the amounts of chemicals measured in the tissues of many whales and finding that local fish could account for only a small percentage of the total. Where the remainder came from puzzled me until I saw a newspaper article about eels caught along the river. They had been banned from the German market because of their high levels of the insecticide mirex, a chemical prominent in belugas, and one that had a single source near Lake Ontario.

Eels enter the rivers and lakes of the St. Lawrence and Great Lakes basin as larvae from the Atlantic Ocean. They remain in the rivers and lakes until they become adult. Each fall, mature eels swim back down the rivers and lakes into the St. Lawrence on their way to the ocean where they were born, to spawn in the Sargasso Sea south of Bermuda. Those that migrate out of Lake Ontario carry mirex and other chemicals that have accumulated in their bodies as the eels fed in the lake. For just a few weeks in October, beluga whales catch migrating eels as they pass through the estuary on their way to the sea. This brief feeding period is sufficient to account for almost half of all the chemicals present in the belugas' blubber. Most of these toxic chemicals have long been banned in North America, but they still circulate through the ecosystems where they were once used or dumped. The Great Lakes and the land that drains into them are the main North American reservoirs for such chemicals. Lake sediments, invertebrates, fish, and birds all hoard toxic chemicals, some of which drift down continuously into the St. Lawrence from Lake Ontario. Every year, more pollutants are added via long-range atmospheric transport from countries that use these pesticides and chemicals, such as Mexico, and even faraway India, China, and Siberia.

From his post on the Rivière-du-Loup ferry, helmsman Girard is a keen observer of life on the St. Lawrence. He knows that the water flowing by his ship comes mostly from the Great Lakes and from the rivers that drain the farmlands and industrial areas of Québec. Like other members of the crew, he is alarmed. He tells me that these days, many fishermen no longer dare to eat some of the fish they catch. But the whales still do, he says, looking at me. *How could they know that the fish are chemically tainted? Even if they could tell that the fish are no good, what else would they eat?* The crustaceans, worms, and organic particles stirred up from the mud by the ferry are contaminated, too. Belugas do not have access to sterilized and toxic-free canned food from the store, although the helmsman is quite sure that the whales often do find empty cans down at the bottom of the river. . . .

We are now two-thirds of the way to the north shore, and the dock at St. Simeon begins to show behind the western tip of Hare Island. The village is perched on the slopes of the mountains, and through my binoculars I can see that the ferry will not be returning empty. The ferryboat veers sharply to starboard around the buoy marking the passage to the other side. This is an area of strong eddies and rip currents that marks the border between the two main channels of the river. There are reefs on either side of the buoy where cormorants and ducks fish during the long summer days and where belugas come in the spring and fall to feed on herring spawn stuck to the rocks and seaweed on the bottom.

All summer, this is a favorite hangout for female belugas and their young. They have long since grown accustomed to the ferry and dive right under it as we churn through the tidal eddies beyond the edge of the shoal. I walk to the other side of the wheelhouse to see where they will surface and find that I am being observed by the two children who were watching me earlier on the lower deck. They, too, have drifted up here and are climbing and peeking over the NO ADMITTANCE sign on the handrail for a better look inside the cabin. Their smiles catch me, and I walk out on the bridge toward them. They know who I am and have come to say that they are brother and sister from Montréal. Their school has adopted one of our photoidentified beluga whales. I remember their school, where I was invited to celebrate their sponsoring of a whale the children named Omega. Pupils from every school in the district had participated in raising money for the whales, selling T-shirts with a custom design. On that day, I had walked through their exhibit of drawings and paintings, listened to songs and poems, and watched a play, all on the subject of belugas. Now the boy and girl want to know if Omega has been spotted this season, and I promise to check with our team working on the water every day out of Tadoussac. They run back to the passenger deck, and as I watch them disappear down the gangway, I know that they hold one of the keys to the future of the whales.

Suddenly the phone rings in the wheelhouse; *It's for you,* says the captain, handing me the receiver. Who on earth would phone me here. I pretend to wonder . . . but I know. The marine operator has a call for me from the *Bleuvet.* A bad omen: this is the name of our research vessel working on beluga photo identification somewhere downstream. This is exactly where I was headed to spend a few days observing live belugas in the wild. Over the phone, I recognize the voice of Daniel Lefebvre, our captain, calling on his VHF. Normally I am tense during these one-way conversations, in which one must wait for the end of the other's message before speaking. But at the moment I am in no mood to say anything. I don't even have to listen: I know what he is going to tell me. He has just found a dead whale in the river, and he is towing it to shore. I will be there in less than an hour. And back on the road to the necropsy room in less than two, with the senseless guilt that comes from driving with a dead whale behind me. I hope it is not Omega.

OPPOSITE PHOTO: Kilt, a friendly juvenile with an injury on its back of unknown origin, was one of the first photo-identified belugas to be adopted. If still alive, Kilt is now a white adult. (PHOTO CREDIT: ROBERT MICHAUD)

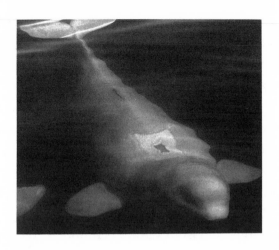

The Afghan Prince

*O*ur world was a vast expanse on which nothing grew and where there were no shadows to mark the course of the sun across the sky. The track of time was easily lost and no record of its history could be found, even though this world was as old as the earth. It stretched away uniformly in all directions, and the unwary traveler lost his way on its unmarked roads. When he tried to retrace his steps, he might have found his previously smooth and easy ride turned into a rough and treacherous journey. Traveling across this world was like treading a path laid out by a fickle mind. Indeed, this realm was but an illusion—a screen drawn over the real world below. It was the mere surface of the world of whales.

Our quest was to understand how beluga whales lived in the St. Lawrence. As an offering, we had entrusted our lives to the river. Ours was a small boat, its crew smaller still. There was Daniel

Lefebvre, captain and master whale watcher, thoroughly calm, reliable, and of the soundest judgment. He always knew how to find his way in a desert or through a storm, whether sand, snow, or water. He spent most of his days standing on top of the cabin, scanning the horizon with eyes goggled against the dazzling sun. When the boat was moving, Daniel saddled himself in a crow's nest built from stainless steel rods bolted to the cabin. With his body and head covered against the wind, and his sharp, tanned features immune to any weather, he looked like a bedouin on his mount.

After all, Daniel was descended from the daring navigators who had come to this land from Europe centuries before. First among them, in September 1535, was Captain Jacques Cartier, who sailed up the St. Lawrence river on his second voyage of discovery to America. Two guides were on board his ship, the sons of a St. Lawrence Iroquoian chief he had captured the year before at Gaspé and brought to the court of France. Now they were showing the Frenchman the way and teaching him about their country and its inhabitants. Cartier wrote everything down, such as the name *Saguenay* for the mouth of a river that cut a deep gouge between the mountains, penetrating deep inland. On September 2, Cartier left this fjord on his starboard side, peering anxiously all around for possible shallows suggested by the low-lying islands and many rip currents. The strong tides and treacherous shoals kept his ship from making much headway upstream that day, and so he set anchor off Hare Island for the night. In the morning, having set sail to the southwest, he found his ship suddenly surrounded by porpoises, large white porpoises, the likes of which he had never seen. His native pilots called them *Adothuys* and said they were good to eat. To the Frenchman, they looked like large fish, white as snow and spotless; and their slender bodies and heads reminded him of greyhounds.

On our own small craft, finding the whales was Daniel's responsibility, and experience had taught him where they were likely to be. Much depended on the tide, which governed the amount of water and the strength of the current on the river. A sharp eye and constant vigilance were required to spot the whales from afar when they came up fleetingly to breathe. When a sighting was made, Daniel directed the boat cunningly to the place he expected the animals to resurface. He might speak to give his orders; more often than not, he resorted to sign language. A raised arm pointing the way, immediately followed by a tap of the heel against the roof transmitted his orders to the helmsman in the cabin below.

That faithful servant was myself, and I thoroughly enjoyed a role that exempted me from having to make any decisions. Steering a motorboat among whales was a much-welcomed vacation from the office and from my usual worries about not-so- alive belugas. At the same time, this trip was a grand learning opportunity for me. Normally, I went on the river for single-day trips each summer during which Daniel was both captain and helmsman, and most of the whale watching on top of the cabin was carried out by our colleague Robert Michaud. As a young biology graduate, Robert had come to my office in Rimouski to introduce himself and to borrow an outboard motor and a camera lens for his study of fin whales in the St. Lawrence. By that time, I had become worried about the belugas, and I was glad to meet someone who might be able to tell me something about live whales in the river. I gave Robert what he asked for in exchange for his keeping an eye open for white whales. He became hooked on belugas, of course, and eventually designed our study program on the whales' live population. Robert was now away in the Arctic, having accepted an invitation to be the whale expert for a crew filming narwhals around Baffin Island. In his absense, I joined this expedition bound for an upstream part of the St. Lawrence estuary where the whales had been little studied. I had signed on enthusiastically, hoping to soak in what I saw indiscriminately, as if I knew nothing about beluga whales.

The other members of the crew were my daughters Martine and Éliane. At twelve and six, they considered themselves old hands, having been on the water with me for various research projects every summer for as long as they could remember. Éliane was the life and soul of the party, ever playing the role of the agreeable extrovert, but deep inside always holding her ground. She thought nothing of making conversation on any subject with someone older than she. Éliane was always busy with something, but she had to surface every few minutes or so for a hug and a kiss. She first met wild belugas when she was four and had been silent throughout the experience, probably considering with much apprehension what would happen if she fell in among them. Nevertheless, upon returning to the wharf, she proved that she had what it takes to become a truly unbiased observer of whales: when her older sister asked her what she thought about the way belugas looked, Éliane simply said: "I don't know, I only saw their backs."

For her part, Martine possessed the more comprehensive approach that came with experience. Practical, precise, and intense, she thought that an order underlaid the visible sequence of events and that the rules governing it could be unraveled. Martine was an avid listener and a keen observer of things and people. She would sit still for hours, daydreaming and patiently collecting the pieces with which she gradually built her own life. Unlike her younger sister, Martine could easily survive a full day on a single big hug. To her, our annual voyage on the St. Lawrence was a ritual in the same category as her birthday and Christmas. On the present trip, she had already become closely reacquainted with some young whales we had seen the previous year. In her order of things, such encounters were normal. After all: these animals were part of the family, and they had been growing along with her.

And finally, there was the Prince, who had become ensconced in the cabin, unbeknownst to the captain above. I had pulled him out of my hat at a point in the trip when something had to be done for the younger of our two deckhands. Spending a week on a small boat involves some measure of boredom, and I could see that the best pages in the coloring book had all been filled and that the even more interesting card game had been overplayed. There were still many hours to come when seemingly nothing would happen on the river, times when the belugas would refuse to cooperate, even if only by showing their backs and thus exposing a piece of the puzzle. These were occasions when I would search my mind for another adventure from the world of the Prince and then take my two young crew members along for a dive. As I spoke, Martine duly recorded my words in her diary so that I could call on her to remind me where to start when I again resumed the story of the Afghan Prince.

The Prince was only a boy when his kingdom in the piedmont of the Himalaya Mountains was destroyed by foreign invaders. His life was saved at the last moment by his faithful aide-de-camp Ibrahim, who took him from the palace shortly before the break of day. Together, they slipped away on the officer's horse, riding toward the sun as it rose over the indigo mountains that marked the frontier of their realm. The day was calm, the ride easy, and the Prince happier than ever, unaware of what was happening to his inheritance. As his story unfolded in my mind while we cruised along, it seemed more and more a reflection of our own innocence, a presage of our own destiny. The river was the kingdom of the whales, but it was also ours. Deep inside me lurked the fear that if we ever lost it, we would find ourselves with no other place to go.

In this fear lay my profound and undisclosed motive for taking this trip. The toxic chemicals and lesions that I had found in the beluga carcasses adrift or washed ashore every year had foretold a bleak prognosis for the population. The condition of the dead animals was a clear indication that something might be wrong with the health of the river. I wanted to see if that notion was correct, if there might not be another side to the story. Perhaps observing live animals in the wild before any one of them showed up on the beach with disease would calm my apprehensions about their survival. I knew what belugas were dying of in the St. Lawrence, but I wondered also how they managed to make a decent life there. Would everything look normal here in their own environment, or would I be able to tell that something was wrong simply by looking at those whales that were still swimming?

From the moment we left the pier at Tadoussac by the Saguenay fjord, I was overwhelmed by the water as much as by the whales. The freshness of the air, the pristine beauty and the silent power of the river subdued me. True, I had to sit alert for hours on the edge of my seat to stay on course while checking the instrument panel and logging the positions of Daniel's observations shown by the Loran navigator. But life often boiled down to holding the wheel with an idle hand, my head poking out in the sun through the hatch. It took me only a split second to leave the boat and queue up with a flock of cormorants or razorbills flying in the distance just above their reflections on the water. The St. Lawrence did not by any means look like a dying river; it was hard to connect my present task to my previous work with whales lying on the shore. I was accustomed to examining a whale by touching it, being able to assess at once its length, color, and sex, and eventually its age, genetics, diseases, and the chemical nature of its tissues. But the live whales were within the river, not on it, as we were. From the boat, although we were often very close to the whales, I could only get glimpses of them.

Whale watching is one of the most tedious of undertakings when your purpose is to understand the lives of cetaceans. It is a game of hide-and-seek in which you rarely see the other team, but they see you all the time. You do not win merely by searching them out and shouting when you glimpse a streaker running between two safeties. You win only after you have understood exactly where the other team was hiding all that time, how they got there in the first place, what they were doing there, and even who was who among them. The belugas had the advantage: they knew we had landed on the top of their world the moment we had left the pier several days before, and they could hear every one of our moves. To add to our frustration, they obviously were not always interested in playing our game.

Fortunately, this was not Daniel's first experience with the river and its inhabitants. He had learned to be humble and patient, and had become attuned to the whales by following their pace. That is why, even though our small boat was not truly adrift, we spent a lot of time drifting. For what seemed like hours on end, nothing happened. Then a whale would burst through the surface like a quantum breaking through time-space, seizing me as surely as if I had fallen unexpectedly into the water. And I was hooked. That single image became imprinted on my visual cortex, as if a chemical were seeping into my neural tissue and making a connection with some fundamental archetypal structure deep inside my brain. I kept searching for a replay of this match as if I had become addicted. Then I understood why Robert had gone in search of the narwhals and why Daniel was on the water day after day.

One becomes willing to put up with rain, fog, cold, and wind in return for those few precious moments when something actually happens. One event out of a hundred may add some new knowledge, lead to an insight, or simply make a feeling of connection with another intelligent being. These are the prizes and more: a whale changing its course to coast slowly toward the boat just beneath the surface, rolling on its back, swimming with head turned sideways watching the people aboard; a cow gliding pure white against the greenish water, passing by with a brown calf sitting on her back, as if on a Sunday stroll; a playful juvenile resting his head against the side of the boat, allowing himself to be gently stroked by everyone aboard. And then they are gone, as swiftly as they have come.

The first night out, we docked at the marina of Cap-à-l'Aigle on the north shore of the St. Lawrence. It was a tiny village with a large herd of summer residents whose main occupation was nurturing their beautifully restored wooden houses. They were nestled on the edge of the rugged Laurentian plateau, which plunged 325 feet deep into the St. Lawrence against the distant backdrop of dusky peaks 3,300 feet in altitude. The village was so steep that from offshore its houses looked like dots painted on a wall. Our boat had entered the little harbor long after sunset in a rather choppy sea, guided by the green light at the end of the pier and lucky to find a docking space among the vacationing sailboats and yachts.

That night in their bunks before they went to sleep, Martine and Éliane talked about the young beluga Pascolio, whom we had seen earlier that day, a few hours into the trip. Pascolio, a young gray beluga whom Daniel and Robert knew quite well, was a hunchback, but otherwise typically playful, an inquisitive and faithful fellow who seemed to recognize our boat from far away and never missed an occasion to come and say *Hello, here I am, I know who you are.* He had been observed many times among different pods of beluga whales and at various sites throughout their range. Whereas most adult belugas paid no attention to the boat—and if they did they usually came only once to investigate—Pascolio often came to visit us several times during our prolonged contacts with his group of whales. He was a familiar sight to our research group; meeting him always had a comforting effect on me.

At sunrise, we left for a potentially productive new whaling ground across the river near the south shore. I took the boat from its mooring through a thick, low-lying fog that masked the frontier where land and sky merged with the sea. I steered carefully among the sailboats seen the previous night but which now seemed to have disappeared, leaving only the tips of their masts suspended in the air. We came out safely between the breakwaters hidden under the mist and cruised unhurriedly over a fresh new sea that nothing had yet wrinkled and that chirped when broken by the bow. We headed straight across the St. Lawrence estuary, around 130 feet deep, bound for the Kamouraska Islands. I was not a little relieved when their cliffs rose in the distance as the sun had started to shred the fog into wisps.

The Kamouraskas are rocky promontories of quartzite at the edge of a milewide flat that dries out almost completely during spring tides. A trough almost two hundred feet deep lies against the islands, a formation that favors a resurgence of mineral-rich deep water, which is always a sign of productive marine life. We had had reports from a local resident that belugas were commonly seen off the islands, an observation that Robert had confirmed during aerial surveys of the beluga range on the river. It was one of the sites that he had selected for our exploratory study of the middle estuary.

We arrived early and started patrolling the sector, ready for a long wait if needed. It was another perfect day, our white little boat coasting on the blue-green water by the rocky cliffs that shone in the rising light. Their summits bristled with spruce trees, from which an occasional great blue heron looked down on us. We drifted through bands of guillemots sitting tight on the flat water as if they had absolutely nothing to do. Indeed, it seemed as if it did not matter much whether or not we would see whales today. . . .

Clang! on the ceiling of the cabin. I poked my head out through the hatch. Daniel beamed at me and invited the crew to look to port 25°. He had finally spotted a pod of whales, and one of them seemed to be a known individual. I steered in that direction, anxious for some action. The game of whale watching becomes even more interesting when you know who the whales actually are. In many parts of the world, researchers have established that individual whales can be recognized. An outstanding catalog with photos of thousands of humpback whales from the seven seas identifies individuals by the patterns of white-and-black pigmentation on the underside of their flukes. Here in the Gulf of St. Lawrence, Richard Sears has put sixteen years of work into a file containing more than three hundred blue whales that can be recognized as individuals by the pattern of pigmentation on their flanks. Theoretically, such patterns allow whale watchers to identify each individual in a population. The situation is different with beluga whales, since adults are a uniform white coloration without shades or tones.

Fortunately, some years ago pioneering observers of belugas in the St. Lawrence noted that many of the whales had striking natural marks. Following up on them, Daniel and Robert spent countless days on the river over three seasons and confirmed that most animals had these marks. Most were trifling nicks and scratches that might or might not be permanent, but there were also more distinctive and permanent marks. These were an assortment of scars that seemed to originate from old injuries, cuts, punctures, or deep gouges into the animals, each of them forming patterns that are very unlikely to be repeated identically a second time on another animal. There were also a number of whales with conspicuous malformations of the vertebral column. Patiently, Robert and Daniel have put together a collection of photographs that enable them to recognize about 125 individuals with certainty.

Presently, Daniel wondered if the marked whale in the pod that we were cautiously approaching was an animal that he had met before. At first, we could see only three whales, then five, and finally six. They were not in tight formation; instead they appeared to simply be hanging around in the same area. It took quite some time before we could ascertain which whale was the one with a mark. Belugas very rarely show their flukes or their heads above the surface, and the only marks useful for identification are those in the middle part of the body, not too low on the flanks. If there is a mark on one side only, we may have to move around the animal—or have him move around us—to see it. Ideally, a whale will have one good mark on each flank. Or best of all, he will have one right near the ridge on his back, since, as Éliane had noticed, that is about all we ever see of a live beluga whale in the water.

After much steering on my part and foxing on Daniel's—he had lifted his four-hundred-millimeter lens to eye level countless times for nothing—we finally got several good views and photographs of the animal with the mark: a rather impressive but thoroughly healed scar arcing across the back, as if a long time ago the whale had had an unpleasant encounter with a sickle. Daniel doubted that this animal had been seen before, and the girls were already busy trying to check it out. Martine was leafing through a green binder lying on the chart table. There, tucked beneath polypropylene protector sheets, were dozens of black-and-white photographs of belugas snapped by Robert and Daniel over the last three years. Some animals had been photographed only once, others several times a year. Ordered in the binder according to types of marks, the photos each bore a numeric code and a date. A number of photos also had names. These belonged to belugas whose marks had a familiar shape or who reminded the researchers of someone or some special event that had occurred in the field at the time. Such were Walter the Waiter, Alpha, Slash, and Pascolio. Still others were belugas that had been adopted and named—such as Omega, Caresse, and Delphine—by sponsors, many of whom were kids of Martine's and Éliane's ages.

Eventually, although Éliane had pointed out a number of animals in the catalog that looked like the one that was just then swimming near us, Martine concluded confidently that this was a new animal—a verdict that Robert would later confirm. By that time, the whale had split from the loose group and Daniel had decided to follow it. Suddenly, we heard an excited shout from the top of the cabin: the whale was a female, and she had a newborn calf with her. That made our day. From then on, and until dusk, we stayed at a safe distance, observing the cow and her calf. He was of a delicate light brown, about the size of the arching back of the mother when she surfaced. When they came up together, his color contrasted with that of his mother, who shone so white under the sun. The pair swam lazily up and down the river along the islands. In typical newborn fashion, the calf surfaced as if he were not too sure about the position of his blowhole. He would lift his head clear of the water, pushing firmly with his flukes, and fall back in stiffly. At regular intervals, the mother would stop short at the surface, floating like a balsam log and looking twice as long as she did during her regular surfacings. While she remained so on the rippleless blue water, the calf would disappear beneath her to suckle for a minute or so. As soon as he reappeared, the pair would resume its idle roving.

That night over dinner, we all felt like kids who had a big secret to tell. Who would have believed that we had spent the day watching a whale nursing her calf off enchanted islands? Everything was so peaceful, so pastoral, the tide changing after six hours just as it was supposed to do, the sun rising and setting exactly where and when predicted, and the whales coming and going calmly in and out of their world, showing no fear of us. The stillness of the water, the day's ending in the soft tones of the sun setting over the mountains, the seabirds sailing back to their island nests—nothing seemed to have changed for eons. Lying in my bunk that night, I could not interpret what I had seen as a sign that the belugas were under any threat.

The following day, we left the islands at midday to head upstream, to cover a number of the sites on Robert's list. We approached a headland on the south shore by the mouth of a small river, where the village of Rivière-Ouelle was founded in the 17th Century. This was one of the main sites where men once set traps to catch beluga whales. The tide was low, exposing a vast expanse of mud and sand punctuated by rocks deposited by melting glaciers thousands of years ago. The warm air rising over the flat under the midday sun made the coastline look higher and closer than it was. I could not locate the cove and the large boulder where the villagers erected the first of the long line of poles that led to the main trap. I pointed to an approximate location, describing to Martine and Éliane how the men built the long weir that stretched offshore toward us. Unsuspecting whales could not have made it out, and neither could the girls. Éliane was apprehensive with the mud and the clam worms that bite the toes. Martine wondered what would have happened to the mother and calf with whom we had spent the previous day had they swum into the trap. I lied, assuring her that the men would have released the mother and her calf unharmed. I resolved that someday I would tell my daughters the true story of one of the hunters on this shore and his young daughter, Marie-Simonne.

For the next few hours, we cruised slowly toward Île-aux-Coudres, an island lying low and close to the north shore. The river is still twelve miles wide in that area, and approaching it from the south, the isle is lost in the grandeur of the mountains. The extensive shallows on the south side are not inviting, and all ships now berth on its north shore. This is where, on September 6, 1535, Jacques Cartier landed after anchoring his three vessels in the relatively narrow north channel. His guides told him about a considerable beluga fishery held every summer by members of their tribe, who came paddling by canoe from their main village near Québec City, sixty-five miles upstream. Following an old tradition, they fished and hunted harbor seals, gray seals, and beluga whales throughout that highly productive region where the river meets the sea. On an island farther downstream, across the mouth of the Saguenay, the remains of tribal dwellings and fires have been found buried under the grass and pebbles. Among the artifacts retrieved by archeologists were teeth of mammals, which were sent to me for identification and aging. A small number were beluga teeth from several animals, both males and females. They were identical to those from carcasses that I have sampled on the beach, and I made thin slices from these fossil teeth to estimate their ages. The animals were eight to twenty-three years old at the time of their death, more than 1,700 years ago.

When he returned to France to describe a possible new passage to India, Cartier vaunted the abundance of whales in the great river. French sailors from the Basque region, who had been fishing the coast of Labrador and Newfoundland for decades, were thus encouraged to go farther west. They built temporary shelters on shore near the mouth of the Saguenay, where they rendered right whales and probably beluga whales as well. They were followed in the next century by permanent colonists, who settled by the St. Lawrence to farm and to trade for furs. By that time, the St. Lawrence Iroquoians had vanished without a trace, but belugas were still plentiful. Concessions for catching whales were made by the king's representative, and in 1721, there were fifteen weir net fisheries on both shores of the St. Lawrence. One of them is said to have been first set on the western tip of Île-aux-Coudres in 1686; it endured until recently.

Cartier also experienced strong and dangerous tidal currents around Île-aux-Coudres. On his next visit, he waited nine days for the river to calm down before he could return to France. The river in that area is a tangle of fresh and saltwater streams, some brownish, warm, and light; others green, cold, and heavy. They do not mix readily upon meeting, but roll over each other, producing broad bands of quivering water, like the rips of a tide that moves over an irregular bottom, even though very deep under there is only smooth sand and gravel. At the surface, the water whorls and simmers quietly in a calm, but the slightest wind will turn it into a choppy sea. These fronts progress slowly upstream with the rising tide, then veer downstream with the combined flows of the river and the tide's ebb. Spiraling at the surface is a mixture of foam, small organisms, reeds, and driftwood from the continent that will have been thoroughly skimmed by an army of gulls by the time it reaches the ocean.

A surface rip continues underwater as a broad vertical boundary between different water masses, and at dusk that day, we discovered that belugas sometimes took advantage of it. We had come near two small groups of whales and let our boat drift toward them. They were swimming on either side of a line of eddies. We soon ended up in the rip current ourselves, moving endlessly in a long spiral within the narrow band of eddies, watching the belugas repeat the same behavior over and over. Each group of five to eight animals regrouped at some distance on either side of the shear zone and then swam toward the others in fan formation. As soon as they got near the rip, they turned around and moved away, only to swim again toward it within a few minutes. We could not see what was happening underwater, but we assumed that the whales were cooperating in herding fish toward the shear zone. The fish presumably got confused and easier to catch when they entered the zone of turbulence.

The next day of our own quest was again a long one, punctuated by stops to watch small groups of whales that were taking advantage of the rising tide to swim upstream. It is when they are traveling that belugas seem to be most intense. Now there was a group coming on the tide toward the boat from behind, as if there were something they had forgotten to show us. They were swimming fast and steadily with a common purpose, and at times surfacing in synchrony, their blows short but powerful, swimming only inches below the surface. At closer range, I saw the tiny waves pushed ahead by their round foreheads just before they broke the surface. As the pod glided by, I noted how long and slender their bodies were, not at all like the rounded and limp forms that stranded on beaches. One large white adult rose higher above water, and I knew that he was checking out our boat when his brown eye met mine.

He was gone in an instant, and I felt the urge to follow. There were so many things that I needed to know from him, and somehow I believed that I deserved more, that I ought to be given some greater reward for my effort. I felt suspended in midair, like a predator in ambush, feeling that ancestral urge to grasp and to control. I strained to see where he would come out again and saw him veer toward us, still at close range, about to break the surface. Daniel's camera clicked, and my heart stopped, as if I had been out on the river with a gunman of yesterday and he had just shattered my world with a simple pull of his finger on the trigger.

We spent a few days near Île-aux-Coudres , navigating outside the buoys that marked the main channel, among treacherous currents that could drive us aground. Nowhere did we see the large herds of belugas that would have been common when the weir nets on the island and on the mainland to the south caught two hundred or more whales each year. There were only small pods of belugas, usually one or two animals together. They came and went, sometimes approaching the boat to investigate but mostly paying us no attention. Several animals with conspicuous marks were photographed, a few of whom turned out to be new additions to our files. At this rate, the catalog would soon hold identification sheets for two hundred animals, and close to one-half of the total wild population would consist of whales whom we knew individually. . . .

On the last morning of our trip, Pascolio came to greet us, his usual self, with yet another group of whales. He swam away from his pod for a few minutes and came right to the boat, passing underneath twice, once swimming normally, and then on his back, belly-up, for all to see that he was a young male. He wore the peculiar beluga smile, that permanent feature of the species that gives it the look of an enigmatic wise man or, rather, of a happy imbecile. After Pascolio had rejoined his group, we left for the marina, where we arrived after sunset. We had reached the end of our quest, and I had found nothing to suggest that all was not well with the belugas that were still alive in the St. Lawrence.

In the soft light of our last night on board, secure at our mooring, I was again spellbound by the silent beauty of the river punctuated by the short blows of belugas passing off the pier. I sat on
the gunwale, happy at last to be in a peaceful state of mind at a
time so serene and on the river so still. I realized how much I cherished my children and the whales, and how precious their world
had become to us all. Daniel was perusing through his field notes
of the day; Martine was writing a last page in her diary, while Éliane
followed suit with her somewhat improvised version, asking her sister how to spell Pascolio and where it was that we first had seen
him. I looked over the water, wondering where our young carefree
beluga, unaware of the turmoil in his world, was roaming tonight.
And though the night was so calm, with the slightest of winds moving about the rigging, and there seemed no reason to suspect that
our kingdom could be lost, I felt a slight twitch of fear inside me.
I knew then that Pascolio was the Afghan Prince.

I climbed onto the pier and walked to its end, where I watched
the sweeping beam of the lighthouse on a spit upstream. The current surged against its rocks and folded into whorls that shone
when they came into the green light of the beacon above my head.
The spirals carried foam, pieces of weed, and other scattered
remains of the life of the river that were exposed at the surface for
a moment before they spun away into darkness. That was all we
had seen of the lives of the whales: bits and pieces skimmed from
the surface of their world. That was as much as we could learn by
traveling on the river for just a few days, observing whales come
to the surface for air.

Though weir nets were no longer set on the shore, whales were
still dying by the acts of man, although the river held no record
of that story. The whales left their world when they died, rising

to the surface, where they were taken up by the whorls of the rip currents to be pecked at by gulls until they drifted onto the shore. It was within their tissues that their history was written, in the many chemicals that had accumulated for decades and had caused physiological stress and health disorders. These were clues that could not be obtained by looking at the live whales swimming at sea, who would breathe normally and look healthy until the last moment. Only when they landed would their secrets be revealed, enabling us to tell what was happening at sea by reading its selected writings on the shore.

Had the St. Lawrence beluga population been followed closely on the river over the previous thirty years or so, we would already know if their numbers were still decreasing or not. As it was, Robert and Daniel had only started their work recently, and it would be years before they could measure the survival of females and know whether they gave birth to a sufficient number of calves to replace the adults and the young that I was picking up on shore year after year. So few people had paid any attention to the whales, even during the last decade, when we had become interested in the living only after the dead had drifted to our door.

I felt a hand touching mine. Martine and Éliane had come onto the pier to join me, and we sat with our legs over the edge, facing the black profile of the mountains against a last fringe of dark blue sky where the sun had set. I could only hope that, unlike the young Afghan Prince, riding toward the rising sun, my daughters would not let so much grandeur mislead them about the health of our river kingdom. Four and a half centuries had passed since Jacques Cartier neared this same spit of land. There were now no new continents to discover, no uncharted seas to explore—only old ones that needed to be preserved, a task for which there is no one to guide us.

Villagers gathered around a dead whale. Rivière-Ouelle, 1920s. (PHOTO CREDIT: FATHER FERNAND BÉRUBÉ)

Skeletons from rendered belugas left scattered on the beach at Rivière-Ouelle. 1920s (PHOTO CREDIT: FATHER FERNAND BÉRUBÉ)

Beluga whale beached by hunters near Tadoussac, 1909. (NEG. # 24365. PHOTO BY R.C. ANDREWS. COURTESY DEPARTMENT LIBRARY SERVICES, AMERICAN MUSEUM OF NATURAL HISTORY) OPPOSITE PHOTO: Children pose for the photographer standing upon victims of the exceptional catch of more than 100 belugas on a single tide at Rivière-Ouelle in the 1920s. In the background are the sheds used for rendering beluga oil and storing tools and dressed skins. All the whales appear to be young adults, possibly from a single herd. (PHOTOGRAPHER UNKNOWN)

Marie-Simonne's War

S tanding still in the mud and sand, twelve men watched the tide rise over the flats. On this calm day of early spring 1915, the river that they called sea was smooth and heavy like slate. To the northwest, it was only four miles wide, abutting a rugged, mountainous plateau with blunted peaks, but to the northeast the water looked infinite. In that direction, the St. Lawrence stretched unbroken all the way to the Atlantic Ocean, hundreds of miles downstream. It was toward that horizon that the men peered in hope over the edge of their world.

They were exhausted, yet elated, by the crisp and moist air that accentuated the feeling of a job well done. They were strong and sturdy men, their short statures emphasized by ill-fitting clothes of heavy country wool and well-worn caps of brown and gray. Hands reaching inside jackets for pipes and tobacco, they smiled at a young lad unable to steady his horse-drawn cart. He was no match for his Percheron, who had become nervous with the change of tide. The horse was digging into the ground with his hooves to pull away, looking back at his inexperienced master with large and soft eyes, begging to return to higher ground. Already, the growing river lapped around a line of long and slender poles that the men had just finished driving into the ground. Within minutes, the water reached the small group of men, wrapping small eddies of whitened water around their muddied boots.

Walking around in front of his horse, the young man pulled at the reins, while the others heaved and pushed at the cart, whose wheel had caught under a large boulder. As soon as the wagon was under way, they all hopped aboard and sat with legs dangling over the sides. They were laughing and joking as they always did when not working. They were teasing Joseph Lizotte, their leader, who was still standing out there near the line of poles with water up to his ankles. His dream had become reality. He had renewed with the old tradition: after years of neglect, he and his associates had set the weir. He could not take his eyes from the northeast, squinting obsessively, searching for some sign of life. Now the whales must come to make it all worthwhile.

Finally resolved that this would not be the day, he, too, waded back to shore. He was greeted on the beach by Marie-Simonne, four and a half years old, the youngest of his eighteen children. She was standing on top of a boulder much bigger than herself, held there by her fifteen-year-old sister. Seeing them, Joseph was angry at Theodora for taking his baby to the river so early in the season. Over the years on his farm by the river, he and his wife had lost six children and infants to disease and to the will of God. But Joseph was immediately appeased by the young child in her little dress and heavy sweater when she jumped into his arms as he walked by the rock. Usually, she asked to be tossed in the air and chuckled and squirmed like a guinea pig. Today, however, Marie-Simonne was silent. She tucked her arms between her own body and that of her father, feeling the rough cloth of his shirt against the back of her hands. She rested her chin on the heavy shoulder, staring back toward the sea at the forest of poles slowly being covered in water. She did not like what she saw.

She did not know how it worked, but she knew it was a trap for animals. She had not yet recovered from the day last week when her brother Roland had caught a rabbit. Roland was mute and, she had been told, could not even walk when he was her age. Yet he had caught an animal in a snare and killed it. Marie-Simonne had tried to bring it back to life by pulling at its eyelids to expose the eyes, and everyone had laughed. They laughed again when she did not want to have any of the rabbit at supper. She did not know how to cope with the stare of animals and thought they were best left alone. Not like her brothers, who, as soon as the snow had gone, were out in the woods, catching and playing with birds, woodchucks, and fish. And they dug for clam worms with which to catch the fish. Looking out at the water's edge, Marie-Simonne thought she could recognize the very spot where, minutes ago, she had been bitten by a worm. All she had wanted to do was to pick up a beautiful red stone, when the creepy blind creature had dug its claws into her big toe. Marie-Simonne had begged Theodora to carry her back to shore, where her sister stood her on the big rock.

The tide now reached the rock, having drowned the near end of the line that the men had set. In all, there were 7,200 maple and birch saplings planted firmly into the silty bottom of the St. Lawrence. The previous summer, Joseph had bought out or joined with the other owners of an ancestral right to set 1,200 stakes each.

Together, they had spent the fall cutting small trees of the right length and girth from neighboring villages. The lower ends had been sharpened and the boughs cut away, leaving only a crown of young branches with buds ready to burst on the first warm days of spring. The trees had been precisely counted and piled on shore before winter had set in. Months later, as soon as the ice had drifted away to the ocean, the men had worked steadily through four low tides to cart the poles out onto the flats and drive them into the ground. They had progressed faster than expected, for they did not have to look long for the best site to set the weir. Even after all these years, men could still find, here and there, the broken ends of poles that their fathers had driven down before them, poking through the soft clay. There were only two low-lying areas, called the "big pond" and the "small hole," where the ground never showed. Today had been the first spring tide of the year, when the river shrank more than usual and only a few feet of water remained in the pond and the hole. It had been the only opportunity for the team to complete the structure before the beginning of the season. The best men had been selected to set the poles down there, and the trap had thus been completed.

Since 1705, this traditional weir had been set near the mouth of the small Rivière-Ouelle, where the tide receded as much as one and a half miles from land over a smooth and gently sloping flat. No one knew where the plan came from, and many thought that early settlers had simply improved on a device invented by St. Lawrence Iroquoians. Its design was ambitious, yet simple; overwhelming on a human scale, but appropriate for capturing giants. First, along a straight line that started some distance below the high- tide mark, eighteen- to twenty-foot-long poles were planted at two- to three-foot intervals. This line was called the "wall." About half a mile farther down, the wall ended in a pen in the shape of a rough half oval. This area, called the "yard," was more than one mile wide by three-quarters of a mile deep, and the poles around it were closer together. There was but a single entrance into this yard, facing the shore on the upstream side of the wall. This "door" was about a quarter-mile wide, and its upstream frame, aptly called the "hook," was sharply bent inward like a gigantic fishhook. To someone flying above the St. Lawrence, the weir would have looked like a gigantic kidney bean, its eye turned toward land, to which it was tethered by the long dotted thread of the wall.

In the early years of the colony, the poles had been linked together by a double row of twine or boughs. Through time, the hunters had learned that the twine was unnecessary for directing the whales along the wall toward the yard and holding them within. The weir was effective for various reasons, the first one being topographical. With the rising tide, a herd of whales would go beyond the flats to enter the mouth of the Rivière-Ouelle in pursuit of fish. When leaving the area on the ebbing tide, the mammals would meet the land end of the wall, immediately veer toward the open sea, and follow the long line of poles into the yard. Even though the distance between the poles was large enough for most individual whales to push their way through, the belugas ended up swimming in large circles, trapped inside long enough for the hunters to arrive and to constrain them until sometimes there was hardly enough water for the whales to move at all.

Even among the hunters, there had always been some speculation about why the whales were fooled by this device. Of course, water flowing out to sea with the tide was murky and sediment laden, and even an animal with keen eyesight would not be able to see the poles. The men had learned that belugas did not rely much on vision, for they would readily approach boats until scared away by sharp noises. The world of these whales was at best one of shadows but above all a world of flowing water, of vibrations and of sound. Belugas were led beyond the trap by their greed for fish, and they were drawn into it and chose not to leave because of their total confidence in currents and acoustics. Busy feeding on fish inshore beyond the weir, the whales would only leave late on the ebbing tide. At that point, their instinct told them not to swim back against the ebbing water but to follow the wall toward the open sea. After entering the yard, they would still not swim back through the door to freedom. At the same time, their senses interpreted the hundreds of stakes vibrating in the water as an impenetrable wall or at least as an unfamiliar and threatening obstacle. And, many an old hunter would insist, the whales were also scared by the shadows projected on the water by the crown of leaves left at the tips of the poles.

Every year, the weir would be set just before the whales came back from their winter quarters in the Gulf of St. Lawrence or perhaps from even farther beyond, in the waters near Labrador and the Atlantic. But in the early 1900s, the hunter's tradition was broken and the weir was not set for the next several years. Now the whale fishery was about to be resumed, and every village on the lower St. Lawrence would remember that year: 1915. This was a year never to be forgotten for another reason, for on the other side of the ocean, the great world war had been going on for months, and in just a few weeks, it would feed on its first Canadian troops. While Lizotte and his men were setting the weir, many young men from the villages along the St. Lawrence were digging themselves into the soggy trenches of Vimy in France, and most of them would find their graves in those muddy traps.

The war had not yet brought sorrow to Rivière-Ouelle. It would be months before the news would first arrive that someone had lost a brother or a son and before villagers would become unable to look at the river without thinking of those who had never returned from the sea. The war was still a grandiose adventure full of hope, glory, and opportunity. At home, it had created a new economy, jolting the demand for all kinds of goods, including whale products. Joseph Lizotte, who was trying to be both a farmer and a businessman, had seen a legitimate opportunity to help his family and his country. He would catch whales as his father had done. He would render the oil, prepare the skins, and ship everything to the ocean terminal at Québec City. Perhaps if he fed the flesh of the belugas to his hogs, he might even ship pork to the city. Joseph had great visions because of the war, and he had prepared well. But he could not foresee that the war would eventually bring something unexpected and unwelcome that he would live to regret.

⟿

*T*he first whales trapped were a female and her young. It was April 25th, and as he did every day, Joseph had sent one of his lads to the shore on the full tide to look out for whales. That day, the boy returned to the house out of breath and excited. There were whales in the yard! The associates were gathered, the horses harnessed to the carts, while workers and onlookers gathered on shore. Theodora was moved by all the excitement and the rush of strong men going to the beach for what seemed like a sacred event. She went with her sister Laurence, two years younger, with whom she spent most of her time, and they took Marie-Simonne along in spite of her cries of protest.

When the girls got to the shore, the men had already killed the whales and hauled them up the beach. The two belugas were lying on their sides among the pebbles, each one tied to a horse with a length of manila. To Marie-Simonne, standing alone on her rock at some distance, they looked like shining bibelots lost on the vast expanse of shore, clean and delicate, like china in the morning light. One was pure white and had what looked like a red collar band around its nape and throat. Next to it was a plump, smaller shape of a strikingly contrasting soft blue-gray. Both had serenely smiling faces and small, wide-open eyes like those of the piglets in the shed behind the house.

The men were saying that this first catch was a good omen from Mother Sea and that their quest would be rewarded. But to Marie-Simonne, it spelled disaster. From then on, she could not quite get her mind off the dead calf, and for weeks on end, she would see him at night when lying in her bed, looking at her with his little eyes. Eventually, she came to believe that somehow this young beluga caught in the trap on the first catch was related to herself.

On May 1st, thirty-five whales were caught in a single tide. The day before, Joseph and his elder son had spent the afternoon by the river, watching whales come and go but never getting close to the trap. There was a strong northeast wind, which people of the river dreaded. Northeasterlies ran all the way from Labrador over hundreds of miles of cold water, building up a big sea and pushing the high tide above its usual mark. Presently, the only white-backs entering the trap were the caps topping the waves. Father and son were having doubts about their weir, thinking that they would have to modify the trap. Then, the following morning, Joseph came back from his sunrise walk to the beach and announced that the sea had calmed and that belugas were entering the trap in droves.

Within the yard, from which the tide had nearly fully retreated, the belugas were all clumped in the deepest part of the big pond. Their big melon heads huddled in the shallow water, their bodies forming a gigantic rosette. They were appallingly easy prey for the men, who went from one animal to the next, dodging the flukes and walking over slippery bodies. They slashed at the belugas with shafts with pointed steel ends, locally known as claymores. A single good strike, aimed a few inches behind the blowhole, shattered a skull, crushing the brain and killing the animal instantly. The men then cut holes through the flukes and tied each animal with a manila. If the tide were high enough, the whales could be hauled out by the horses. But presently, the water was too low, and, as usual, the horses refused to go beyond the first sand bank. Anchors were therefore tied to the carcasses to hold them until the tide returned and the bounty could be brought to the stubborn horses with rowboats. The men walked back to shore for a smoke, but some of the children stayed awhile, sitting on the whales and feeling the skin, smooth as cellophane, until their feet were numb with cold and the rising sea lapped at the shoes they had left high on the beach.

At high tide the following day, the horses strained to drag the heavy carcasses up the beach over rocks and sand. Once on shore, one man, using a long knife, would slit a whale along the spine from fluke to melon and then all along the belly. Helpers with hooks then pulled at the heavy skin and blubber mat while the first man sheared them off the carcass with short strokes of his knife held against the dark muscle mass. He worked his way from one end of the whale to the other, carving a single hole around the base of the pectoral fin. The animal would then be turned over and the men would proceed in the same way with the other half of the body. This heavy mat of hide and blubber, known as the bonnet, was then dragged by a horse to a shed beyond the beach grass at the edge of the woods. In the meantime, the workers on the beach kept busy cutting most of the muscle mass off the skeletons, to be ground and lightly cooked into a kind of rillettes to feed Joseph's pigs.

At the shed, one end of the bonnet was nailed to a roller set on a rough trestle and slowly wound up while the blubber was scraped off the hide. This was done with hurried strokes of a sharp knife, which here left a fringe of fat on the hide and there cut halfway through the leather. Large slabs of quivering fat fell on a couple of rough boards under the trestle. One man removed any strand of flesh still adhering to the blubber and then cut the slabs into smaller chunks, which slid on their own greasy oil down into a half barrel. Two men then pushed a stick through facing holes across the lip of the half barrel and carried it inside the shed. The heavy load of blubber was dumped into a grinder that delivered cubes of fat to a boiler. Scarcely any heat was required to obtain beluga oil, for the fiberless blubber was so soft that it would start liquefying on its own in the sun.

The raw hides now had to be dressed. Some blubber was still attached to their insides, and a uniform layer of denser fat, the delicacy called *maktak* by Inuits in the Arctic, still adhered to their outsides. The hides were folded over once and buried in the sand to cure. When retrieved after a few days, they steamed like horse manure. The smell was horrible, so they had to be cleaned in open air over a couple of beams. This was done by the hardiest workers, who hurriedly scraped away the grit and what was left of the rotten *maktak* and blubber with a garden spade. The hides were then covered in salt, folded over again and stacked in barrels.

Every month or so, barrels of oil and barrels of hides were carted from the beach shed to the wharf a few miles away, on the other side of the bay. They were loaded onto the slow wooden riverboats that ferried logs to the mills and other goods upstream to Québec City. That first year, a total of 105 belugas thus found their way into the world economy. Joseph's house and those of his associates had a pungent new smell. Their work boots and clothes were forever stained and impervious to rain and snow. The path leading from Joseph's barn to the river was strewn with pieces of boards, odd tools, and broken cart parts, all permeated with beluga oil. The track opened onto a section of beach that looked like a disaster area. Whale oil glued pebbles and sand together, forever sealed lichens onto their rocks, and stiffened the blades of the beach grass. Below, near the water's edge at the high-tide mark, 105 plundered and unwanted carcasses were slowly rotting. The stench kept Marie-Simonne away from the river all through the summer and fall.

Marie-Simonne had become an outcast. The girl had no resources of her own and found no support from her brothers and sisters in her private battle against the killing of belugas. She rejected anything that had to do with the dead whales. She would not eat the doughnuts that her mother cooked in the specially prepared, clean oil from a fresh young beluga. She would not touch pork meat, either, because the hogs were fed on whale meat, and she eventually scorned fish, too, because they were the innocent bait that attracted belugas near shore to be caught in the weir. She did everything she could to be sent to her room at mealtimes, to avoid her brothers' main subject of conversation: how one of them got thrown into the water by a fighting whale. How they dunked the neighbor's boy into a barrel of whale oil. How the carriage horse of the parish priest could not be coerced into the stable because the other horses inside smelled of whale meat and blubber. That same smell also had killed in Marie-Simonne the urge to cuddle in her father's arms. And now in her room, she saw the sadness in his eyes glowing on the wall next to those of the beluga calf.

⤳

*E*arly in the spring, the trader from Québec City who bought the barrels of whale remains came to see Joseph Lizotte. Mr. Canac-Marquis had brought with him the proceeds from the last shipment of the previous fall. He had come to tell Joseph that this year, he wanted him to be more careful with the hides, explaining that he could obtain better prices in England if they did not have as many nicks and blade marks on both sides. He showed the Lizottes a sample of boot laces made from genuine beluga leather, as well as a piece of fine tanned leather, smoother than cowhide, almost without grain. He also explained that they could obtain oil of a much higher grade by rendering the blubber immediately after the whales had been killed. As it was, the oil from Lizotte's operation sold for only twenty cents a gallon because it was often of poor quality. Mr. Canac-Marquis specifically recommended that Joseph prepare the oil from the melon separately and showed him a sample of fine, odorless melon oil that was used in optical applications. A small bottle of this clear liquid fetched one dollar in New York City. Joseph listened attentively, but he told the man from the city that his associates had their own uses for whale products, that everyone here was also busy with farming, and that he knew no one would be convinced to change his ways of doing things.

Marie-Simonne listened, too, and understood that the hunt and its horror would be on again this year. She had prepared for that eventuality over the winter and had thought out a plan to save the whales. She would get into the yard before the men and let the belugas escape. To accomplish this, she had to be up very early in the morning and get to the beach. Then she would wait for the tide to go down, take her shoes off, and walk to the weir in the mud. To her, this was the hardest part of the plan. She would have to get used to the cold mud and to walking among the clam worms lurking beneath in the dark. So she practiced that same week when no one was looking with a bowl of chocolate pudding that her mother had put in the icebox to set . She dipped her toes in, feeling the cold substance squirt as she pressed and wriggled. Then she tried to imagine that there were clam worms in the bowl, *real worms*. But that was too much, and she pulled her foot right out, spilling chocolate pudding all over the floor.

But Marie-Simonne was still only a little girl when the belugas returned from the gulf that spring. She could do nothing to prevent dozens of whales from being caught in the weir. The beach once more was no longer a place to walk and to look for shells and nice stones, no longer the place where the day ended on a rock with the sun setting over the mountains across the river. It was a battleground. The family home once more became haunted with dead whales around the kitchen table at mealtimes and when the hunters smoked after supper and the neighbors came to chat. One evening, someone told a story that Marie-Simonne liked very much, and she would ask her mother to tell it to her when they were alone in the kitchen in the daytime.

The story said that many years ago in their village, on the June 24th national holiday, a phenomenal number of belugas had been trapped in the weir. People had come from all the neighboring villages to celebrate the day and to marvel at the miraculous catch. A dancing party had been arranged in a huge barn on a spit of land by the shore where the whales lay, waiting to be carved up the following morning. Hopeful about the profits to be reaped, the villagers had brought in substantial amounts of rum, whiskey, and wine, which kept them up and lively late into the night. Their songs and music could be heard at the edge of the forest behind the village and out over the bodies of the whales, which shone in the moonlight and against which the rising tide had started to lap. Shortly before midnight, as the fête was reaching its peak and everyone was dancing in the middle of the room, a dancer saw fleshless hands come out of the walls and stretch out as if to seize him. The hands disappeared instantly but sprung out from another corner of the room. Before long, many others saw more ghastly hands, and within seconds, everyone ran out of the barn into the brisk air by the shore. There, they found with dismay that the high tide had lifted the beluga carcasses and carried them some distance away. The evil spell continued shortly, when strokes of moonlight reflected by the waves turned into human ghosts that slowly rose up to ride the whales. They brought their mounts back to life, and the whales' eyes shone like bright coals, and their blows spat flames as they swam away into the night, leaving a swarm of phosphorescent trails. For many years afterward, no one dared return to that stretch of shore.

Increasingly now, the evening conversation switched from the killing of animals to that of men in their own trap in Europe. As she sat quietly listening until she was told to go to bed, Marie-Simonne tried to imagine how and why the men were fooled into the trenches and whether or not they drowned there. She did not understand how they died—whether they were hit in the back of the head when not looking or something with huge pincers caught them by the foot in their sleep. She could not understand why they never tried to escape and what the purpose of it all was. She never heard anyone say where the bodies went, or what they were used for.

In the fall, belugas always became scarcer. The fierce storms of September, surging on the tail of faraway tropical storms, drenched the trail and the seagrass. The high winds and frightening waves churned the beach and brought up a layer of fresh sand and pebbles. Then, around the end of the month, in a single night the tide rose very high under the bleaching light of the full moon. The sea almost covered Marie-Simonne's rock and rose all the way to the shed at the edge of the forest. When the tide retreated in the morning, the carcasses of the summer had been taken away to the bottom of the sea. This marked the start of Marie-Simonne's season. The belugas, both the living and the dead, could rest in peace, and she could go back to the beach. By then, the sun at noon had become soft and warm, and for a while it seemed that a new summer would start right away and everything would be fine.

In winter, the kitchen resounded only of the war, and Marie-Simonne became sad for the soldiers, who were always in season and could never rest in peace. She saw that many a neighbor who came to the house to talk was also sad, and she understood that some of the men who were trapped in Europe were from her own village. And then the following fall a few soldiers came back, and the neighbor's elder son was among them. He was to come to the Lizotte house one night when the kitchen was packed with villagers to hear about the events overseas. Marie-Simonne sat tight against the posts of the handrail at the top of the stairs to the second floor. When the soldier arrived in the yard, there was a hush through the room, and Marie-Simonne went to watch him through the window of her parents' room. The soldier was missing a leg and pounded on the boards with his crutches all the way up the steps onto the verandah and into the house. He seemed very sour when he talked that night at the table, everyone around him listening, ill at ease, without a word. But Marie-Simonne simply thought he was fortunate to have escaped.

That night, people said that the war would be over in a few weeks and that their other sons would be back soon. The season, it seemed, was indeed over for the men as well, and during the next few weeks, almost every day there was news of more returnees. There were many others who came back missing a leg or an arm, or an eye or two, maimed and forever sour about something that could not be undone. Others returned with a respiratory disease from which few recovered, and they did only after passing the germs on to their own people who had stayed at home. It was a form of the dreaded influenza virus known as the Spanish flu, and it was deadly. It had already struck all of Europe and flown around the world. It spread like the high tide across the land, reaching into the smallest and faraway villages. It found its way into Joseph Lizotte's house and into the lungs of his youngest child.

No one knew how to treat patients and how to prevent the spread of the disease. People stopped kissing and would not even touch each other. The parish priest believed that poultices of cooked onions were very effective for curing the sick, and Marie-Simonne's mother had her daughter wear one around her neck. The little girl was put in isolation on the second floor in a large, windowless recess near the stairway. The space had been furnished with a small bed and her own belongings, and the entrance to it was closed off with a blanket nailed to the ceiling. From within, the girl could only follow the pace of life downstairs by listening to every sound and feeling the vibrations with her fingers against the wall. Most of the time, lying in her bed breathing painfully, she felt she was drowning like a beluga in the weir just before being hit by a spade. She knew that she was meant to be sacrificed in exchange for the young beluga killed three years before, in the first spring of the hunt.

She clung, however, to the belief that if time would only run, if the tide would turn, if she could save but one whale, the spell would be broken. She had to get to the beach, walk along the wall, enter the yard, and . . . She did not have the strength to do it now, but next spring, she would be almost nine years old and a big girl. Fortunately, it looked like the whales had already left for the winter. Nothing would happen today, anyway. She had heard the church bells volleying frantically. It must be the call for Sunday mass. Yes, she kept repeating to herself, it is Sunday morning, and no one will be working on the beach. Such a fine day, too. She heard the swing squeaking under the maple tree and her brothers chatting on the verandah, rapping the backs of their chairs against the cedar siding. Downstairs, dishes were being set on the table by her sisters for a midday dinner. No. The dishes were being washed . . . and it must be afternoon. Or night. But why were the church bells ringing?

That is when she heard someone yell the dreaded call, like a gunshot, announcing that belugas were near the weir. The front door with its creaking spring banged several times against the jamb. Shouts and steps moved swiftly around the barn, and a rustle flew and faded away along the path to the beach. The house was suddenly mute, and Marie-Simonne knew that it was too late. In her condition, she would only get to the beach after all the animals had been killed. This meant that she had to die as well. Peering at the wall, she summoned the glowing eyes that had scared her awake so many times. When they materialized, shining like bright coals, she remembered the story about the whales brought back to life, and she resolved to go and ride one away. She got up ever so slowly, her head throbbing, and dressed up in her best clothes, leaning dizzily against the wall. She went downstairs, found her way to the front door through the dazzling light, and started down the path to the beach.

It was midafternoon, and the air was very warm for this time of year. Marie-Simonne could hear the slightest movements of the grass under her feet, of ants climbing up on twigs, and of the mellow breeze coming in from the south between the rows of spruce trees bordering the lane on either side. Silence was buzzing all around her, but she could hear nothing in the direction of the river, no shouts of excitement, none of the usual calls between men and horses at work. She hurried as much as she could and came out in the open by the beach. It was covered with whales. They seemed to have come in scores right up the shore on their own. Everywhere she could see there were white hazy shapes lying peacefully on their sides. She did not see the horses and the hunters, she did not see the weir. There were only strangers in their Sunday clothes walking among the bodies, touching a beluga whale here and there, as if they had never seen one or would never see one again.

In the middle of this herd of ghosts two young boys, all dressed up, stood still on top of a whale. In front of them, on a rocky ledge overlooking the beach at the water's edge, Marie-Simonne could make out the lower half of a man behind a tripod, his body hidden under the black cloth wrapped over a camera. Next to him stood a figure in a white Sunday hat. When she came closer, she saw that this was Joseph Lizotte, her father. Solemnly, she walked to the little boys and she climbed on the whale next to theirs. Looking at her father and at the camera, she waited for the miracle to happen. It was November 11, 1918—Armistice Day.

Marie-Simonne died in her bed at sunrise the next day. When Joseph saw his wife's eyes as she came down from the little cell upstairs, he walked out the door to the beach. He sat on Marie-Simonne's rock, looking out to the edge of his world, pondering the price he had paid for his contribution to the war effort.

OPPOSITE PAGE, PHOTO CREDIT: PIERRE BÉLAND

Code Name DL-8-93

*I*t is ten at night in the small agricultural town of St.-Hyacinthe in the heart of southern Québec. At this time of the year, it has been dark for a while and evenings are always cold, whatever the weather. My windshield mists up as I slow down to make a right turn into the driveway. The headlights sweep over a blue sign with white lettering that says UNIVERSITY OF MONTRÉAL—FACULTY OF VETERINARY MEDICINE. I drive around the main building and park near a street light against the brown brick wall under a NO PARK-ING sign. I look around for a few seconds before I get out of my car. I am expecting a visitor, and all I have to do in the meantime is to stand there, yawning, hands dug into my coat pockets, while the street light keeps watch on another blue sign with neat white letters: NECROPSY [Autopsy] ROOM.

On the other side of the lot, there is a stable where farm animals are kept under observation. Some are main characters in research projects on animal diseases. Others are valuable breeds with ailments or are animals recovering from operations. I walk to the large open door to watch a thoroughbred horse neigh, his hooves loudly clomping as he is walked into a stall. The horse turns his large, frightened eyes toward me just long enough for his trainer to pull him in. The stall is tidy, and its sliding door bears the animal's name and that of his owner under a clear plastic cover. Next to it hangs an aluminum binder that holds a file describing the history and prescribed treatment of this patient. The stable is warm and cozy, with a few dozen animals—cows, sheep, and horses—in as many stalls. Good night.

I slip out of the animal hospital on the warm air that is gently flowing into the frosty yard. The chill outdoors reminds me that the patient I am expecting, although also a large mammal, will be as cold as the night. It will have traveled many hours on the road after having drifted on the river for who knows how many days. My visitor will be dead. It is the corpse of a beluga whale, and I have his file under my left arm. It holds nothing more than the initials of my patient's scientific name, the Latin words for "a white dolphin without a fin," *Delphinapterus leucas.* DL.

I look up for the thousandth time at the huge indigo doors on the opposite side of the lot. Behind them is the animals' morgue, and that is where I shall spend the night. The doors are wide enough to let a dinosaur through, and they are made of heavy metal panels spanning the height of the building. Next to them, a notice posted on the wall reads LEAVE YOUR ANIMALS HERE with an arrow pointing down to a green fiberglass bin. That is where you drop your dead cat or dog if it happened to die after hours and you do not feel like keeping it at home until daybreak. If you also leave your name and address, your pet will be taken into the necropsy room in the morning, and you can phone in for the verdict and the bill.

The place looks as strange now as when I first saw it ten years ago and every other night since. Ever since my student years in another university, I have found campuses somewhat unreal: is there another place that makes one wonder so intensely about one's raison d'être? I remember walking through an empty parking lot after cramming till midnight for a test, feeling as though I was leaving a place that had been closed down and abandoned years before. True, there is always a night watchman on the other side of the building. Although he does make regular rounds in between TV programs, perhaps his main role is to make believe that the campus is still alive. Here, shortly, we shall get a whale inside his building without his noticing a thing.

Through a lighted window on the second floor that I had not noticed before, I can see the shadow of a human figure against the blinds. Probably a graduate student working through the night, slowly becoming mad. But here I am in the dark, myself, waiting for a dead whale three hundred miles from the sea. My breath condensing in the halo of the street lamp tells me the air is getting colder still. My fingers are getting numb, and I feel like some new species: *Homo apterus*, man without hands. Helpless.

My inner wanderings are brought to an end by the familiar spluttering of a diesel engine—to me, the unequivocal call of a dead whale. The street lamp has also caught the scene: blue truck, brown trailer, white whale. The convoy rushes past me and stops abruptly in front of the animal hospital. Then, trailer and whale first, it backs down the ramp that leads to the entrance of the necropsy room. How clumsy and out of place this bleak animal looks, stretched out in a low and narrow trailer custom made to fit him! Yet the corpse gives meaning to my night. And to Richard's, for

he has just spent ten hours behind the wheel with a pack of cigarettes. To him, this is but one event in a long day. He will leave
again for home on the lower St. Lawrence with truck and trailer
as soon as the autopsy is over, in four to six hours, depending on
what we find inside the body.

When I greet Richard, I sense a sadness in him, and I share
it, for we used to comb the beach for whale carcasses and truck
them together. We are both traveling alone now, missing the friendship that brings laughter and comfort in the night when it strikes
you that the road may not have an end. I break the ice by telling
Richard how privileged he is: when he gets back home, he will have
completed half of the tour of the Gaspé peninsula in less than
twenty-four hours. Many workers from this small country town
spend half their summer holiday doing just the same thing.

The limp body of the whale appears to be somewhat bloated,
yet it smells relatively fresh. Richard wraps it up tightly in a strong
web of net and twine, while I go through the big blue doors to
fetch the electric winch. Once inside, I smell the familiar odor of
the spotless necropsy room, a mixture of asceptic soap and the scent
of dead flesh. Holding the control unit in one hand, I walk the
powerful tool all the way to the end of the rail that juts out of the
building like the arm of a crane and let it hang right over the trailer.
As soon as Richard is through with his packaging, he hooks the
end of the winch chain into his spider's web. I press my numb finger into a rubberized button on the control unit, and like a wiz-
ard, I slowly lift the whale. The motor rattles and strains audibly,
and we fear it may not be able to lift the body clear of the platform. But we make it by an inch, and the whale registers at 2,866
pounds. Male.

Carefully avoiding the door jamb and maneuvering around the
bends in the hallway, I slide the prey inside, leaving a trail of blood

on the concrete. The rolling lift struggles and clatters until the whale rests precisely over the blazing stainless steel necropsy table, which sits a few inches off the ground. Only then do I notice on the other side of the table, half hidden by the hanging whale, several human figures in white coveralls who seem to float vertically above the dark red floor of the floodlit room. I bend down and turn my head sideways to have a look at their faces. Among them are my colleagues Daniel Martineau and Sylvain De Guise, both veterinary pathologists. Sylvain joined our team some years ago as a student, and he likes his work so much that I never feel guilty about waking him up for a cadaver in the middle of the night. He is attended by a pod of students who have never seen a whale and who keep their hands securely tucked away inside their spotless smocks. More apterids.

Richard and the vets orient the leviathan along the axis of the table, and I again use my magic wand to set it down. The whale slowly sinks onto the table, flattening like dough in its net until it almost overflows on either side. Then, with a lot of heaving and pushing, while the electric motor refuses to pull another inch, we manage to retrieve the net from under the whale without seeing it literally spill onto the floor like some alien blob. It is a fine, huge specimen, fourteen feet and three inches long, too long and awkward for the table. The snout juts over one end, while the flukes and some of the tail stock hang down over the opposite end. It is now obvious to everyone that necropsy rooms are made for things more familiar. Preferably the size of a horse or smaller—like pets.

The whale is hosed down to wash away the sand and grit from the beach and the road. We are busy for a while taking standard measurements and photos, describing marks and scars for identification purposes, and examining any lesions on the skin. As usual, there is no evidence of foul play or accident that could have caused the death of the whale. We deliberately mark time during these proceedings, as if we are about to embark on a hazardous trip. Some of the neophytes in our pod do not know about this and assume we are taking a well-deserved break after the exhaustion of setting the whale on its coffin. But now the time has come to find out what the whale died of, and we should now be stripping the blubber away to look inside it. Yet we are halted by some unspoken rule, as if required to pay respect to an animal of the sea secretly spirited away to the confines of the earth. Or possibly we know that what we will find inside may be incriminating and held against us.

No magic formula will open a whale, and only through strenuous effort is one led to the organs that carry the message. I learned how rewarding this undertaking could be on that fateful afternoon in September 1982, when on the beach, with the lighthouse at Pointe-au-Père as a lamppost, I touched my first beluga whale. I was immediately fascinated by the insides of this organic torpedo, the organs that kept it moving, breathing, perpetuating itself, until they had suddenly stopped working. I discovered how the science of the pathologist, explorer of the microcosmos, allowed him to decipher the message written within the tissues—how he could sometimes interpret accurately the color and pattern of spots on the liver, like an ancient Roman priest reading the auspices. The pathologist's purpose is not, however, to obtain the consent of the gods, but to determine what in the machinery of the cells has gone wrong and caused death.

Animal Number One had also been a male with not the slightest trace of a wound. But I must say, with some shame, that he was to me more of a curio than a patient. Running my fingers over his body, covered in a transparent skin like plastic wrap. Gently pressing on this gossamer membrane of cells covering the delicate *maktak* that protects the true, leathery skin under it. And wondering how thick a layer of pudgy blubber there was over the body proper, over the real animal of muscle and bone well below, protected from the cold waters it used to swim in. Back then, I had no experience with whales and could not even locate such standard whale paraphernalia as the pinprick ears or the mammary glands. I could not tell the sex of a whale unless I made a thorough search for the proper organs. I had never seen a whale that close.

A beached beluga on the St. Lawrence is a media event these days, but it was not so then. Because scarcely anyone paid attention to the whales that lived in the river, there was even less concern about how many died each year. Of course, the stranding of one of the larger rorquals would create a sensation. Such sudden interest, however, would be directed toward the size of the animal, the oddity of some part of its anatomy, the way it had been struck by a ship or caught in a net, or, finally, the manner in which it could be disposed of. Somewhat like a dead moose sprawling on the top of a car, or a panicky deer that must be shot because he is in someone's backyard pool. An animal must go to great lengths to turn its death into an event. Not so for humans, who can almost be assured that each death will be duly recorded.

So beluga deaths went unnoticed, and those that drew attention were hardly considered as useful statistics. The couple of carcasses that were reported each year were considered banal by the authorities responsible for the management of the whales. Don't they all have to die someday anyway? But being only amateurs, Daniel Martineau and I did not know anything about these facts, and we got so excited with our first carcass that we started looking for more. We found out that they were much more common than previously thought and have since recorded 180 deaths altogether. Tonight, we are no longer naive, for we are about to carve into our sixty-eighth beluga whale—the eighth brought to the necropsy room this year. We call him DL-8-93.

Leaning on the table, I press the blade of my knife against the carcass, which lies on its left side. Slowly, I seesaw a cut all along the midline of the carcass, starting ventrally at the throat and running back through the navel and beyond to the anus. I then repeat the procedure dorsally, from the midline of the peduncle forward through the dorsal ridge, which bears no fin, and all the way to the blowhole. We work on this exposed half of the whale only, cutting several lines across the body, vertically through thirteen centimeters of blubber down to the muscle. Then, one hand pulling at the skin with a butcher's hook, we separate the blubber from the muscle with careful strokes of a sharp knife. Painstakingly, we strip large slabs of skin and quivering blubber weighing tens of pounds each off the whale and put them aside in empty forty-five-gallon steel drums. When this long and exhausting assignment is done, one of the students fits a chain with hooks into facing holes across the lip of each of the overflowing barrels and lifts them with the winch for weighing. The total pudgy mass registers at 617 pounds. To this must be added an equal amount to account for the other half of the animal resting against the table. Finally, the combined skin and blubber of this beluga amounts to 43 percent of its total body weight. This is the same as can be obtained from any beluga whale from the Arctic, showing at once how substantial blubber mass is in the species, and, more significantly, how normal and healthy this particular animal would appear to be on that basis alone.

Instead of a white whale, we now have a dark red, quite smaller, nondescript cadaver before us. The rib cage as usual shows through thin muscle, but the abdominal cavity bulges somewhat. Is it bloated with gas or is there something else? The carcass must now be elevated so that we can delicately remove the layer of muscle and expose the internal organs without bending over for the next few hours and straining our backs. Someone presses the button controlling the two hydraulic pistons at the ends of the necropsy table. The carcass moves up in slow motion, while the pistons hum in stereo, producing the very same sound as the huge spaceship that gradually fills the opening screen of a *Star Wars* movie. We sense that this is the beginning of a long night. I do not say anything, but I have seen this bulging abdominal condition before. When the table stops at its uppermost position, I press on the belly of the whale firmly with both hands and let go. A gurgling sound like that of water moving about inside a sealed container fills the room for everyone to hear.

When Sylvain punctures the bulge and cuts through the overlying muscle and tissue that line the abdominal cavity, liquid pours out—liters and liters of a yellowish clear liquid only slightly tainted with blood. I look at Daniel and say the word *peritonitis* with barely a question mark. Ever-doubtful scientist Martineau's answer is a rather affirmative *perhaps*. I look at Sylvain: his eyes are as approving as his reputation will allow. The belly of the whale slowly collapses as the inside pressure is released with the outflowing liquid. We cut away the muscle sheath to expose a smooth lining, the peritoneum, which holds the internal organs together within the abdomen. In this case, it also held all the liquid inside. Removing most of this tissue reveals the stomach and the contorted mass of the intestines, like a heap of oversize sausages. They are a glassy gray, starkly different in color from the pinkish beige of other organs and tissues within the abdominal cavity. The pathologists point to extensive and abnormal growths in the form of filaments adhering here and there onto the surface of the intestines as well as to the veil of connective tissue that holds them together. We observe more of these tangled strands of filaments on the internal surface of the peritoneum. We hold our breaths for a second, for we know that we have found something significant here and that we will very likely be able to tell what caused the death of this animal. It is one in the morning.

As we proceed with the autopsy, the pathologists collect small square pieces of tissue from every organ. They are dropped into jars—thoroughly cleaned and recycled peanut butter, strawberry jam, and mayonnaise jars—filled with crystal-clear formaldehyde. The liquid instantly preserves the tissues in their present state for later examination under the microscope. When blown up a hundred times by the lenses, the arrangement and structure of the various types of cells will confirm whatever preliminary diagnosis is made tonight on the basis of the external appearance of the tissues. What we have just seen in the belly of the beluga—the liquid, the growths, the ashen color of the intestines—are highly suggestive of peritonitis, an inflammation of the peritoneum. Some agent had caused the surface of most tissues and organs within the abdomen to react. Adjacent blood vessels had become permeable, leaking liquid into the cavity. This process must have been going on for some time before the animal died: every day, more liquid was being drawn in. But nothing could control whatever was causing the inflammation. The whale suffered intense pain.

Both pathologists are now searching feverishly for the agent, for the foe that could not be defeated. Delicately looking at every fold of tissue, into every nook and cranny around the gut, near the kidneys, under the liver. Suddenly, it is there for all to see. One of our hands, exploring within the mass of the intestines, has touched something firm and irregular. Carefully shifting the overlying segments of the rolling mass of seventy-foot-long gut, we expose a striking piece of intestine, a site where the surface of the gut is constricted, wrinkled, and folded down from all sides toward a central scar surrounded by small bulging masses. A larger mass protrudes from under the tract opposite the scarred tissue. The diameter of the intestine running up from this site in the direction of the stomach is rather large; down from the scar, in the other direction toward the anus, it is much smaller. Sectioning the tube above the scar and exploring inside it with a blunt instrument confirm that the gut is so constricted at this site that it is almost completely blocked. After carefully examining and photographing the digestive tube in that vicinity, the scar, the masses, and the surrounding tissue are cut away. With a scalpel, an incision is made in the main mass, right through to the other side beyond the constriction. Agent of death.

Inside this lump, the intestinal tissue is hardly recognizable. Instead of distinct and concentric layers of cells forming a hollowed cylinder, one sees a thickened slab of almost uniform texture. Through the center of the mass, a narrow slit is all that remains of the tunnel through which food should normally travel along the intestinal tract during digestion. The mass appears to have grown in all directions, around and into the original tissue. The use of a microscope would later reveal that it was only a nondescript accumulation of disorganized cells and small, tangled blood vessels. The mass had undoubtedly started as a microscopic aggregation of cells that had gone mad and had divided uncontrollably. In reaction to this invasion, the inside lining of the intestine, following the program written in its genes, kept laying down new layers of cells. Gradually, the original architecture of the tissues had been altered beyond recognition, and the open space inside the tube had grown smaller and smaller, blocking the normal flow and interfering with the nourishment of the whole body of the whale. It was a slow death.

All this while, abiding by no rules, following no plan, and growing faster than any other tissue, the mass had organized its own life. Like an army of barbarians taking over some fertile territory, without any control, without any purpose. Tricked by the action of some secret mechanism or ancestral substance produced by the invading mass, the whale had helped it grow by providing a lifeline of blood vessels that brought food and oxygen to this alien body. In doing this, the unfortunate beluga had prematurely fixed the date of its own death. It had proved impossible for the organism to grow such complex and evolved structures as blood vessels fast enough to nourish the ever-growing army of primitive cells. Gradually, outlying bundles of cells and others within the main lump had died from lack of nourishment. Still others had been killed by white blood cells, which produced a toxin to neutralize and kill the tumor. This normal defense mechanism of the body had been insufficient, however. In time, poor health, malnutrition, and the natural toxins produced by decaying cells and white blood cells all contributed to the inflammatory reaction inside the abdomen. The peritonitis seen earlier tonight was but the tip of the iceberg. Something else had been working undercover, something that had sentenced the animal to death. Cancer.

⌐⇁

*I*t is now four in the morning. I am standing by the wide-open indigo doors, looking at the dark red floor of the necropsy room. Richard walks by like a zombie, carrying a heavy orange wooden casket with tools and assorted gear to the truck. Inside the building, Sylvain has just finished rinsing the floor with a hose as big as a firetruck's and he is spooling it back on its rack against the wall. A last trickle of aseptic suds is flowing into the grated trough that runs down the middle of the floor, draining any remnants of blood and tissue to the underground filter below. The place is clean and empty again; the necropsy table is silent, resting against the floor and shining like a mirror. A beluga has vanished, most of it as cut-up pieces dumped into forty-five-gallon drums, the rest a fleshed-out vertebral column hanging in the cold room. It is headed for the recycling plant along with a cow and a couple of dogs examined the previous day, which have already received their own verdicts. All that will remain of our passage here tonight are a number of samples for chemical analyses and tiny pieces of each of the beluga's organs sitting like courtroom exhibits at the bottoms of a few dozen odd-shaped jars.

I walk halfway up the ramp and stop by the truck to try to imagine a line-up of the sixty-eight beluga whales from the St. Lawrence that have passed through these same doors over the last ten years. There were males and females, mostly mature animals, with an occasional juvenile. There were a few small enough to be carried in one's arms and laid down like pets on the necropsy table. Collectively, these animals have added many names to the list of diseases now known to occur in cetaceans. For the record: three of them had spleens blown up like small footballs and as hard as rocks, a condition whose cause remains a mystery to this day. Stomach ulcers were found in many, and a few animals had died when such ulcers perforated, releasing acid digestive fluids into their abdominal cavities and producing fiery reactions that led to hasty and painful deaths. But perhaps the most striking observations were those of tumors, like the one seen tonight.

Worldwide, a grand total of seventy-five tumors were reported by the various professionals who, over decades, have performed hundreds and hundreds of necropsies on whales of many species from around the world. Exactly twenty-eight of those tumors, or more than one-third of the world total, were found in the sixty-eight St. Lawrence belugas that were brought to our own autopsy room. Eleven of these twenty-eight beluga tumors were cancerous, an overwhelming number! This is a rate of incidence much higher than in human patients in health care centers around the globe, and higher than in most of the domestic animals pampered enough to be taken to veterinary hospitals like this one. The intestinal cancer seen tonight in beluga whale DL-8-93 was the third case of this type of tumor from the single small population of belugas that lives in the St. Lawrence. I wonder how I should feel about the fact that such a high incidence is exceeded only in sheep that browse in pastures profusely treated with herbicides in New Zealand, halfway around the world.

As before, I expect that our chemist colleagues in the laboratory will find in the various tissues of tonight's whale the metabolized remains of benzo[α]pyrene, one of the most potent carcinogenic molecules known to science. This chemical is released when organic matter is burned, such as in forest fires and cigarette smoke, as well as in numerous domestic and industrial practices. There are measurable amounts of it throughout the St. Lawrence system, but it is found at much higher concentrations in an area near the center of the belugas range. That hot spot is the Saguenay fjord, downstream from a huge aluminum plant that has been spewing the chemical since the 1940s. Benzo[α]pyrene may well be the direct cause of the observed high incidence of tumors in the belugas. It is, however, quite possible that there is a more complex mechanism underlying the development of tumors in these whales.

In our effort to learn as much as possible about the beluga whale during the autopsies, we had also collected small samples of skin that were sent to two laboratories for genetic analyses. The preliminary results from these samples showed that beluga whales in the St. Lawrence have traits that are not found in other populations. This would suggest that there is little exchange of animals between the Arctic and the St. Lawrence and that the latter form a truly distinct population. The samples also showed that St. Lawrence belugas share some genes more commonly than do those in one Arctic population. If consistent, this would mean that the St. Lawrence animals are more closely related than are belugas from the other localities in the north. Such genetic resemblance among individuals might include the sharing of traits that impart greater susceptibility to particular toxic agents.

I know very well that, in addition to carcinogenic substances, we will find a variety of other toxic chemicals in the tissues of DL-8-93: several dozen altogether. Prominent among them will be lead and mercury, which cause behavioral problems in man and animals, and insecticides such as DDT and mirex, as well as the industrial chemicals known as polychlorobiphenyls, or PCBs. The last three are man-made chemicals with an organic skeleton of carbon and hydrogen, two of the building blocks of life, but to which one or more chlorine atoms are attached. That is why they are known in the trade as organochlorines, and there is an increasingly abundant scientific literature on their varied and deleterious effects. Their general mechanism of action is to disrupt the regulation of the genes' activity. Upon entering a cell, the organochlorine binds to a receptor and joins with proteins to enter the nucleus, where they bind to the DNA strands. The binding of this complex may activate or deactivate a gene, resulting in an excessive production of one protein or a shortfall of another. Unlike the natural molecule that would normally have turned the gene on or off, the toxic organochlorine is long lived, and its action will be felt for inappropriately long periods of time. Thus, a single organochlorine molecule can continuously disrupt the physiology of a cell.

Perhaps the most far-reaching effect of organochlorines is their role as suppressors of the immune system. Like the night watchman to whom you must show your ID to enter a building, the immune system is basically the recognition system that guards an organism. When presented with an object, it gives one of two answers: self or nonself. Self objects are cells or parts of cells that originate within the organism itself, and they will be allowed to move around freely. But nonself objects, such as pollen grains and viruses, or cells, proteins, and membranes of foreign organisms, trigger an immediate response. In a large organism like a human being or a beluga whale, this response is a very complex procedure. It involves a number of proteins and different kinds of specialized cells that are themselves produced and stored within various organs. Their respective roles are to identify, capture, kill, digest, or excrete foreign bodies.

During our long nights around the necropsy table, we have observed lesions consistent with an impairment of the immune system in St. Lawrence beluga whales. For example, the majority of our patients had infections due to bacteria, viruses, and other microorganisms that are opportunistic and will attack only weakened animals. Some of these infections were very specific, previously reported exclusively in old people and thoroughbred horses, both notorious for their weakened immune systems.

Organochlorines can act at various points along the normal chain of the immune response. For example, they are known to modify the ability of a specialized group of white blood cells, the T-cells, to recognize foreign invaders. They may also reduce the efficiency with which another group of cells, the macrophages, can engulf and destroy such invaders. Organochlorine chemicals may also reduce the activity of natural killer cells, whose role is to destroy malignant cells originating from tumors, a condition that facilitates the development of cancer.

I watch Sylvain push the bolts that lock the metal doors of the morgue, knowing that this area of research has now become his major thrust and will be for the next few years. Last summer, he collected blood and tissue from belugas harvested by Inuit hunters in Hudson Bay. I know that in a few hours he will be back in the lab, where he is culturing these tissues and is preserving in the deep freeze billions of beluga white blood cells that will spring back to life when thawed. These are his whale spare parts, awaiting to be exposed to toxic chemicals in laboratory dishes. He is confident that we will get our answers and that we will someday obtain incontrovertible evidence of the chemicals that caused the death of whales like DL-8-93.

Many other belugas that spent their last night as whole whales at the University of Montréal had other health problems of equal significance—conditions that may not necessarily have led to their deaths but that may have influenced their whole lives and have had dire consequences for the survival of their population as a whole. These belugas had lesions on their endocrine glands, small organs that produce and deliver hormones to the bloodstream to regulate metabolism, growth, and reproduction. Here again, organochlorines may have been involved, both while the glands were developing in the fetus and later as they interfered with the glands' normal regulatory functions. The structure of some organochlorines is indeed similar to that of hormones and is thus recognized by natural receptors that transport hormones. Once they become bound to the receptors, organochlorines will interfere with the receptors' normal role of mediating the action of hormones. In our dead whales, there were often nodules, abscesses, and cysts, and one case of goiter in the thyroid gland, which, hidden below the mouth at the base of the neck, produces secretions that greatly influence growth and development of the body. There were cysts and tumors as well in the adrenal glands that sit on top of the kidneys. These glands produce a group of hormones that are important in regulating the salt and water balance of the organism, emotional stress, and steroids related to sex hormones.

Speaking of sex, tonight's male, like other males examined before, did not seem to have had any reproductive problems, or at least none that would have been obvious in a dead animal. Of course, under the circumstances, sperm motility was not measurable. As far as sperm counts are concerned, who knows what the acceptable standard for successful reproduction is in belugas? Some years ago, we found a beluga who, on account of its size and external appearance, looked like a normal adult male, but who on the table with his belly open, turned out to be a hermaphrodite. It could clearly be seen that he had the reproductive organs of both sexes: along with normal testicles and penis, he also had a uterus and ovaries. This is an extremely rare occurrence in nature for a higher vertebrate. Something must have happened while this animal was a fetus growing inside his mother's womb. . . .

As for the females that have lined up on this ramp, they were pitiful. More than half had lesions on their mammary glands in the form of bacterial infections, cysts, or tumors. Some were lactating, a rather clear indication that they had recently given birth, but none would have been able to properly feed their young. Or they would have done so only at the cost of excruciating pain. There is evidence, however, that pregnancies in the St. Lawrence may not occur as frequently as expected. A few females had tumors on their ovaries, and the rate of recent ovarian activity in others appeared to be low. In the animals that we examined, the number of actual pregnancies was much lower than in belugas that lived in the Arctic. True, these females were not healthy and perhaps not as likely to have become pregnant, but reproductive problems are among the known effects of ingesting organochlorines. An experiment in Holland with captive seals demonstrated that animals fed North Sea fish containing the same toxic chemicals as St. Lawrence fish did not reproduce. In the end, this may prove to be the biggest threat to our beluga population. Surely, like any other species, all belugas now living in the St. Lawrence will eventually have to die. If in the meantime, however, they do not leave enough offspring, the population itself will die out.

Feeling cold again as the sun is about to rise over town, I wave to Richard, who is leaving with the truck for a long, solitary drive to the lower St. Lawrence. When he disappears behind the building, I glance at the window on the second floor. The light behind the blinds is now out, and I wonder whether the human figure up there has found his own answer. For my part, I know that I will be coming again to this haunted place where my emotional self wants to split from my intellect.

I walk to my car parked by the street light and feel the pain in my lower back as I bend to sit behind the wheel. Starting the engine, I notice that the windshield is fogged up. I will have to wait awhile before leaving. I dwell again on tonight's death: who is to blame? Lead comes mostly from past use of leaded gasoline. Cars like this one do not spew out lead anymore, but they did for a long time. I am thirsty and glad to find a tin of apple juice on the passenger seat. Apples, until very recently, were grown extensively with the use of DDT to control pests. Well, here is one lead to the culprit: someone who drives a car and eats fruits and vegetables. Most people I can think of fit the description. . . . I look at my face in the rearview mirror. Surely, no one has touched as many dead whales as I have.

Childishly, I trace the letters DL-8-93 onto the glass, wondering whether this whale without a name will be missed by anyone. The hermaphrodite's code was DL-2-89, but his name was Booly. He had been photoidentified the year before by Robert Michaud and Daniel Lefebvre, who were studying the lives of beluga whales on the river. It is a pity that he died, because he had just been adopted and named by a child who lived in Toronto. Booly was twenty-six when he died. I never met the child, and never knew how old he was, and tonight I wonder how he is doing.

The engine is now running smoothly, the windshield has cleared up, and I back away from the wall as my headlights flash on the green bin that says: LEAVE YOUR ANIMALS HERE.

OPPOSITE PHOTO: Juvenile breaking the surface very abruptly upon meeting another group of belugas. Although usually very smooth and nonchalant, the beluga whale is capable of energetic movements and speed swimming. (PHOTO CREDIT: ROBERT MICHAUD)

In the Hands of Progress

I press my forehead flat against the side window of the small airplane. My neck is sore from looking down and back, and my eyes sting from peering intensely at the river three thousand feet below. I lean back with a headache, satisfied that this time I have made a thorough count of the pod of belugas as they have came up to blow by twos and threes. They are tiny at this distance, but their white shapes stand out clearly against the deep blue sea. I give my count to Robert Michaud, who is sitting up front with the pilot. Almost simultaneously, I hear Daniel Lefebvre, who sits next to me, and Martine, who is crouching against the hatch door, shout their own counts over the engine noise. Twenty-one, twenty, twenty-two. Robert has twenty-one also. This has been our largest group so far today.

Banking, the plane makes a last pass over the whales, and I grab my binoculars for a closer view. The animals have slowed down and are coming to the surface all at once. They are pure white and all the same size, eight bunched up like sheep almost on top of one another; and the rest are scattered in the rough shape of a cross, like escorts around an admiral ship. They are shaped like early monoplanes, with stubby vestigial wings on either side of the pilot's cabin. Their rounded heads seem like a last-minute addition plunked onto the front for spying purposes. I had learned from examining dead belugas on the beach that big adults with such broad chests and shoulders could only be males. Presently, three whales arch in a half roll onto their sides, obviously to let an eye and ear point at the source of the noise above.

After circling over the pod a few times to allow any submerged animals to be counted, the aircraft resumes its straight course toward the south shore. We have now been in the air for three hours, except for a short refueling stop, and are completing the last of our lines that criss-cross the summer range of the belugas in the St. Lawrence. We try to fly this grid every other year to find out where the groups of whales are and how many animals are in each group. And in the end, we add them all up to obtain a total number of whales. Although not a true estimate of the actual size of the population, this total has become an assessment of how stable it is through time.

The grid is covered by two planes working together. On the morning of a windless and sunny day in early fall, two crews leave the airfield near Murray Bay on the north shore and fly northeast toward the central portion of the beluga habitat. The meeting point is over a rounded rocky island where Basque whalers used to land in the sixteenth century to render whales. The islet is remarkable for its dense cover of skinny and bleached spruce trees, which make it look like a fossilized porcupine. After a last look at each other and the usual thumbs-up signal, the crews go their own separate ways. One plane covers the upstream half of the grid, while the other runs the downstream lines. It is tedious work, but we have turned it into a challenging game. Only one person in each plane writes down the numbers. Bets are on the table as to which plane will have seen more and what the final tally will be. We only discover these facts after returning to the airfield at midday, when the two leaders compare their data.

The throbbing in my head calms down when we finally come over land. The pilot veers to starboard and increases his speed for the long flight upstream to the airfield. He is in his own world, listening to the traffic in the area through his headphones, though I know that his own bet is in, too, for he has been flying our team for some years and has become fond of us and our whales. Next to him, Robert looks very pleased with the survey. Robert and I understand each other well, having traveled the whole province together to convince industrialists to fund our research programs on the endangered whale. One night, lying quite depressed on our beds in a cheap motel by the highway, I had told him how low I felt being locked in such a place on my birthday. He answered that it was his birthday, too.

Robert is already adding up the figures in his field notebook. He keeps only the highest counts from the two most experienced observers. I lean back on my seat, enjoying such moments when my work is done and I can go back to watching the river. From above, it is like looking down at a map, not at the true world, but at only a representation of it. The shore is still, serene, and pristine, as if people have moved out, leaving only a scar here and there. The path of a power line across the forest; a narrow road leading to a tiny wharf built of Meccano pieces. Around the pier and all along the shoreline of gray rocks stained brown with seaweeds, the dark water is neatly set like a pane of opaque glass on a scale model. When we fly over the pod of whales again, they do not appear to be swimming, only fading away behind the glass in slow motion. A few other whales flash here and there as we go, and I close my eyes, trying to imagine the myriad that would have sparkled on the river when man first flew over it. I try to recall how, in a strange and unexpected way, the fate of the belugas in the St. Lawrence was linked to the early days of aviation.

On April 24, 1928, a small airplane flying over southern Québec was engulfed in a white haze in the fading light of the late afternoon. From the open cockpit, Charles Lindbergh peered anxiously through the snow flurries at the hilly ground, where dark patches of forest showed from time to time. According to his chronometer, he should have reached the St. Lawrence close to Québec City, the end of the last leg of his nonstop flight from New York. But what had started as an easy trip over new territory had become a troublesome adventure. After crossing the border into Canada, his Curtis Falcon had been thrown around by a storm over the northern Appalachians and the St. Lawrence Valley. Lindbergh felt with his hand for the pouch next to him, hoping that the jolts of the plane had not damaged the bottles of serum stored in a case inside.

And then, in an instant, he was under clear skies over the majestic river. He had come out of the clouds right in midstream, as often happens in the St. Lawrence, where storms that blind one shore leave the other unscathed. All along the horizon ahead stretched the rounded forms of the Laurentians, a resilient plateau of formerly mighty mountains eroded by glaciers. The pilot thought about how, less than a year ago, peering this way in hope of seeing the coast of France, he had been thoroughly thrilled at seeing the land. Today, there was none of the elation of having made it first, only the fear of getting there too late.

Leaving to starboard the Île d'Orléans and its neatly ploughed fields poking through the snow, the pilot veered toward Québec City. While his craft banked, he noticed small white shapes bobbing at the surface of the river. At first, he took them for chunks of ice caught with foam and flotsam between wind and current until at closer range he realized that they were moving on their own, like some species of large white dolphin. They were moving beneath him in a determined yet unhasty and graceful movement downstream, their progress clearly visible underwater during their shallow dives. For as far as he could see on both sides of the plane, there was a huge herd of them split into dozens of small pods scattered near shore.

In a few minutes, Lindbergh was over the city, gliding toward the Plains of Abraham just beyond the walls of the citadel overlooking the river. Guided by rows of lights positioned for the occasion and watching for patches of snow, he made a perfect landing among the cheers of a thick crowd come to see the most famous person on earth. But this was no time for socializing; somewhere in this historic old town, Lindbergh hoped that Floyd Bennett was still fighting for his life.

The week before, Lindbergh had seen the message flash at all air fields: BREMEN FLIERS DOWN IN LABRADOR! For the first time, a plane had crossed the Atlantic from Europe to America. The German *Bremen* had left Dublin on a favorable wind, but a storm midway had blown it off course far to the north. At daybreak, instead of seeing New York City in the spring, the crew found itself looking at a bleak winter landscape. After two days in the air and almost out of fuel, they noticed a lighthouse sticking out of the ice like the funnel of a sunken ship. They headed straight for it and made a crash landing on Greenley Island in the Strait of Belle Isle. Their emergency message had been received on April 14, 1928, when it was believed they had been lost at sea like everyone else who had attempted to fly to America from Europe.

Commander Richard Evelyn Byrd had sent to the rescue a tri-motor Ford airplane identical to the one that was being readied for his own expedition to Antarctica. His pilots, Bernt Balchen and Floyd Bennett, also famous for having crossed the Atlantic, left Detroit on April 20th with replacement landing gear and special benzol fuel. Bennett was very sick with influenza, and Balchen piloted the plane the whole nine hours to Murray Bay on the north shore of the St. Lawrence, northeast of Québec City. Upon landing, Bennett was diagnosed with pneumonia and transferred to a hospital in Québec City. The following day, Commander Byrd arrived from Boston to comfort his pilot, and Clarence Chamberlin, also a conqueror of the Atlantic, came in from Hartford. Finding their friend in dire straits, the Americans sent an emergency request for the serum that Lindbergh brought in. But on the following morning, after two days on the brink of death, Floyd Bennett passed away.

Meanwhile, Balchen had flown east to Greenley Island. He was greeted by a Québec pilot named Louis Cuisinier, who had arrived on site a few days before, determined to salvage the German plane. Upon hearing of all the commotion in Québec City, Cuisinier could not believe the turn of events that had brought together the most famous airmen of his time and had put him right in the center of the action. As a youth in France, watching Blériot build and fly the first monoplane across the English Channel, Cuisinier had developed a compulsive desire to fly. After the Great War, in which he became a hero in the French air force, he emigrated to Canada, where he formed with associates the Canadian Transcontinental Airline company. Its planes showed that mail could safely and reliably be carried year round to isolated settlements on the sparsely populated shores of the Gulf of St. Lawrence. That was precisely where the *Bremen* had just landed, yet another proof that airplanes were about to revolutionize society. Cuisinier firmly believed that the world of tomorrow belonged to those who controlled the air, and he would soon find a new way to demonstrate it.

During his mail runs and through the weeks he spent on Greenley Island and the mainland across the narrow channel, Cuisinier was impressed by the difficult life of the gulf's inhabitants. Geography, climate, and the lack of roads isolated them from the mainstream economy, and seal hunting in the winter supplemented their only other source of income, fishing. The productivity of their fishery had been legendary among the European flotillas that had exploited these waters for centuries. Presently, however, it had dried out. The previous year, there had been no cod and no salmon on the north shore of the Gulf of St. Lawrence. Along hundreds of miles of coast where dozens of small communities depended on them, the fish were gone. And the fishermen knew for a fact what the cause of this disaster was: the beluga whales.

Although these white devils had always been around, the fishermen now claimed that they were arriving in droves every spring. There was no doubt in their minds that the belugas were eating and chasing away the cod and salmon. For some time already, the desperate fishermen had been pressing the provincial legislature to act, sending angry messages from their faraway land of granite and stunted spruce trees. And now, when the first flying machine ever to reach America from Europe had landed precisely in their own backyard, they found new and unexpected support. Louis

Cuisinier had heard their complaint and he would soon become their staunchest ally in the war against the whales.

The first phase of that war had already been scheduled to be waged that very summer of 1928, under Colonization, Mines, and Fisheries Minister, the Honorable J. E. Perreault. His strategy relied on traditional methods. Winchester rifles and ammunition were issued to all active fishermen, each one also receiving a stipend of thirty dollars a month for taking a gun on board to ensure that he would shoot any belugas that came near the fishing grounds. This was a well-organized campaign, with an officer in charge recruited in every community. The frenzy reached its crescendo in the village of Rivière-au-Tonnerre, where the parish priest, Father Garnier, was a vocal and proud pioneer of the North Shore. He was the man chosen by the government to be in charge of the war in his own theater of operations. It was Father Garnier who received and distributed to his congregation the goods and allowances for the war, which, in addition to the regular fare, included a special fund of five thousand dollars and personal bonuses for his own services. Perhaps this may have had something to do with the fact that he had added a verse of his own to the regular Litany of the Saints recited in his church: *From the belugas, deliver us, Lord!*

In the midst of this guerilla war, plans were drawn up for intensifying the hunt further and for providing facilities for the use of whale products. One scheme involved equiping a small vessel with a reduction plant and using a flotilla of boats to bring carcasses in. Another strategy addressed land-based operations, and the ministry hired Joseph Lizotte, father of Marie-Simonne, whose weir fishery far upstream at Rivière-Ouelle was still operating. In August, Lizotte was sent on a voyage by sea to identify the best spots for setting weir nets. In a small settlement aptly called La

Baleine, he found abandoned buildings and sheds that had formerly been used for cutting up and rendering large whales. There were shallow mudflats in the vicinity, and Lizotte instructed fishermen about weirs, even determining the exact number of stakes required at each location. The captured whales would then be floated to the old whaling station to be skinned and rendered, a more profitable and sensible way to get rid of them than simply killing them outright. Joseph was a meticulous worker and did a thorough and honest job. His bill for surveying and planning amounted to only $218.50.

To the frustration of Lizotte the following season, none of his plans materialized, for in the provincial capital, Louis Cuisinier had not been idle. His salvage of the *Bremen* had made him a local celebrity, and he was fully committed to the development of a new air transport company, Laurentian Air Express Limited. Over the late summer and fall, he had observed the behavior of beluga whales, noting how they often traveled in tight groups, swimming head to tail in arrowhead patterns like birds in migration, or in more compact diamonds like fighter planes going to combat. Pods could be approached quite easily by air from behind, a tactic that could not be achieved by boat. Cuisinier figured that the whales had poor eyesight and that even though they could hear boat engines at long range underwater, they would only hear the louder sound of his plane briefly when they surfaced. The former fighter pilot practiced slowing down; and, losing altitude, he would get his plane quite close to the animals before they took notice of him. The belugas then fanned out their flippers and turned their heads sideways to look back, like marathoners assessing their lead, losing momentum for an instant as a result of the change in the aerodynamic posture of their bodies in the water.

The pilot had also spotted a number of shoals around the mouths of tributaries, on islands, and elsewhere along the coast where the whales seemed to rest for hours. In such areas, he could circle over the animals without scaring them away. The belugas would dive with a certain nonchalance, as if to hide in the shallows, although their slender white bodies remained clearly visible. And when they left, Cuisinier could follow them for miles into the open sea. Overall, they appeared to be slow-moving and rather unconcerned animals, and he had good reasons to think that his plan to eliminate them completely from coastal fishing grounds would work.

At about the same time, a cabinet shuffle in Québec City had produced a new minister, Hector Laferté, who was hailed as a model politician, young and extremely popular. Like thousands of people in Québec City, he had seen the *Bremen* exhibited at the agricultural fair the previous fall, when 1928 had been declared "Aviation year in Québec." One of his first moves in his new position was to adopt Cuisinier's strategy for applying the powers of modern technology to the solution of an old problem. The minister found the occasion for announcing the plan at a gigantic rally held in Drummondville in honor of his recent nomination. Laferté's own oration stressed the commitment of the government to improving the lot of workers and farmers, a promise that in his rural riding, far from the sea, must have been well received. He then announced that high on his list of priorities was the war on belugas, which was about to take a new turn. The hunters hired the previous year would remain on payroll, he said solemnly, but in addition, starting immediately, the foremost public enemy would be bombed by airplanes.

Cuisinier was anxious to get started and immediately carried out tests with bombs and torpedoes over the St. Lawrence near

Québec City. His first reports were very optimistic, claiming that the noise of the underwater explosions would scare the whales away forever. But the much-publicized campaign was delayed week after week, apparently because the bombs exploded too far underwater. When new triggering devices were installed by the supplier, Canadian Explosives, the ensuing explosions near the surface were judged much more spectacular. On August 7, Cuisinier left for the lower North Shore to set up his base at the village of Havre-St.-Pierre, the main community on the more isolated stretch of shore where the whales were reputed to be particularly vicious and numerous. The site was also quite removed from the eyes of anyone in the capital who might raise objections to what was, even for the times, a rather drastic wildlife control measure. According to an anonymous journalist from Rivière-du-Loup who was the only reporter to cover the war with a critical eye, there actually was an embargo on news from what he called "the front." Very little ever was reported of the actual battlefields and of the number of casualties of the war on whales.

The front was an exceptional landscape of limestone islands lying close to the mainland, and its buff-colored cliffs gave warmth to an otherwise bleak coast of gray granite. The islands rose out of the deep in huge piles of fine-grained stone gently dipping toward the open waters of the gulf. On their windward shores, the sea had laid beaches of polished shingles over extensive reefs where seals basked at low tide. On their leeward coasts, the islands ended in sheer cliffs echoing with busy colonies of seabird nests. Today, they are part of the Mingan Islands National Park, whose offshore waters, now totally devoid of beluga whales, are one of the world's outstanding summer feeding areas for blue whales. It must have been so in August 1929 as well, although the local interest in wildlife was then directed toward its poten-

tial for human consumption, killing white whales being the order
of the day.

J. Hector Vigneau, lighthouse keeper and companion of puffins
on Parakeet Island, lived right in the center of the action. He was
the only eyewitness to have recorded events of the war, in a few
short, matter-of-fact sentences in his diary. The day after
Cuisinier's much-publicized departure for the front, a single entry
in Vigneau's handwriting mentioned an airplane overhead. It flew
toward the southwest, in the direction of Father Garnier's church
in Rivière-au-Tonnerre; and somewhere beyond Parakeet Island,
it launched a bomb.

Imagine the impact of a bomb in this setting. On any given
morning, before the first breeze is up, banks of fog hover over the
channels between the islands. The blows of minke whales and the
hollow sounds of their powerful breaths resonate in air saturated
with water. A light swell comes in from the gulf, and a pod of
belugas materializes briefly through the haze and disappears again
into the long folds of the sea. Later into the morning, the fog lifts
by the cliffs, and the gulls and nesting seabirds cackle as the day
slowly matures into a full August noon. The sun gets hot, but the
water is still cold, dark blue, and sparkling with life. Offshore,
scoters and eider ducks snooze on the silky water, and flocks of
cormorants and puffins go by in every direction, all looking for
fish. Beyond them is the coast of Anticosti Island, crystal clear,
twenty-five miles away.

And then rises a hum that turns into a roar when the small
airplane comes flying just above the water at low speed. The pilot
in the cockpit wears his brown leather airman's hat with the straps
unbuckled beneath his chin. A man crouching in the open hatch
on the side of the aircraft holds a heavy metallic object in his arms.
Then a dark streak flashes through the air under the plane and the

bomb sinks into the sea, exploding in a shower of water and foam. There is an immediate rumble inside the rock face, followed by a sharp but small bang carried on the slight breeze from offshore. It rebounds off the cliff from which the birds have flown in haste, and there is only the dribble of sand and pebbles dislodged from unsure rocks. The sound of the explosion fades away fast, but the underwater world has been devastated. A bubble of deafening sound has expanded in all directions from the explosion, traveling six times faster and farther than in air, numbing fish, birds, and whales, killing whatever higher life happens to be too close to the point of impact.

The plane came back in the afternoon, but Vigneau did not see it launch anything. From the top of his white-and-red tower, the lightkeeper saw a boat chasing a pod of whales toward the mainland less than four miles away: two men and their elder sons in a wooden boat powered by a two-piston inboard engine and a square sail to save on fuel. Men who had been unsuccessful in their summer fishing but luckier in the seal hunt the previous winter. Men at ease on the sea, one of them standing in the bow with a foot on the gunwale, ready to kill not in self-defense, but in cold blood, in a deliberate and methodical way, without second thoughts. And their sons, already grown up, without knowledge of the difference between killing to survive and killing to plunder, clutching government-issued Winchester rifles, their coat pockets full of ammunition. These were men living as their fathers did, in ways not to be questioned, the hunting and slaughtering of wildlife being at once religion, culture, and a matter of taste.

The leader in the bow spotted a whale and directed the skipper to bring the animal into shallow water close to shore, where it could not dive very deep. Belugas are slow swimmers, but the chase was a drawn-out affair, for the men knew that if they got too close, the whale would unexpectedly turn around and sneak beneath the boat to resurface far away offshore. The gunmen wanted to confuse the animal and tire it, and the boys hit the water with oars when the whale turned the wrong way. The shore was near now, and the boat came closer to the frightened animal, which was traveling a few inches under the surface. The whale sped up for a moment with a few rapid beats of its flukes, which brought water boiling to the surface. Then, as it lunged up to blow, it slowed down slightly, looking sideways toward the boat.

The four men had already shot several rounds, not afraid to squander ammunition, for they had been given plenty. Two bullets hit the sides and back of the whale, slashing at an angle through the blubber, touching no vital parts. But the skipper was a sharp-shooter, and he hit the right spot just behind the blowhole with a bullet that left a red blotch where the skull was shattered. The whale stopped almost instantly like a heavy piece of wood, and floated there on its side, a fine specimen that would no longer eat fish. In just a few seconds, it sank slowly, before the men had time to retrieve it. They knew it would be found in a few days, bloated and decomposing, when the wind would carry it to shore. The skipper pulled at the leads to the sail and took the boat home on the wind. At his feet, lying in the bottom of the boat, was the gunmen's dinner—two ruffled eider ducks with limp necks and five rigid puffins with their grotesque parrot bills.

Two weeks after the start of the bombing, Honorable Laferté sat on the deck of the North Shore and Labrador coaster, about to leave Québec City for a long tour of the settlements whose exotic names kept flashing on his desk—Shelter Bay, Magpie, Natashquan, Mutton Bay, Blanc-Sablon. In a file prepared by his aides, the minister leafed through articles about the war on whales in the major daily, *Le Soleil*. He was glad that his party controlled this paper and that only brief and positive articles had been printed. Next to a short piece was an ad for Château butter that featured a drawing of a plane and stated that the vaunted loaf of cow fat had been tested with the same care as the crafts used for transatlantic flights. Laferté felt uneasy, for he was having second thoughts about his involvement with Cuisinier.

He looked at the strong current whirling against the docks at the foot of the promontory, on which stood the historic citadel and the gigantic Château Frontenac Hotel. The minister hoped to find the time to come down to the river in the spring when the whales sometimes swam up this far. Presently, he could imagine them only through the grievances of the fishermen and the newspaper clippings. Famished monsters, wicked breed, destructive fish, ravenous giants, voracious cetaceans. A nuisance; at best, useless animals. Indeed, the grants given by his ministry for boats, fishing gear, wharves, and local roads had not been very productive on account of the lack of fish. The minister was well aware of the hardships of people on the coast, and the policy of his department to subsidize fishermen to hunt beluga whales stemmed in good part from the need to provide families with some cash to help them survive over winter. The prognosis for the coming months was not good, even for people of some wealth like the minister. The whole world seemed to be on the brink of a financial crisis. The front page of an early August paper in his file carried a headline about the New York Stock Exchange, which had been jolted by its most dramatic fluctuations in years. Giants like U.S. Steel, American Can, and Westinghouse had been among those hardest hit.

Laferté got to the briefing notes about Cuisinier's activities. They said that amazingly, after only two weeks of bombing, the whales had left the coast and the cod had started to come back! In fact, since surveys had never been carried out, the minister doubted that anyone knew how many whales there were, and what damage they may have caused to the fisheries. The wisdom of the time was conveyed in another article asserting that at least one hundred thousand belugas roamed the St. Lawrence every year. Each one of those whales was said to feed on one hundred pounds of fish per day, which, over the six-month season, amounted to a total of two billion pounds of fish!

We now know that this was an impossible figure. Recent estimates have shown that there were at the time fewer than ten thousand beluga whales in the St. Lawrence, each consuming a more modest twenty-five pounds of fish per day. The whales' total consumption during one fishing season would then have been less than 23 thousand tons of fish. In comparison, for the year 1929, 43 thousand tons of fish from the Gulf of St. Lawrence were sold on the market by Québec fishermen. It is likely that an equal share was landed by the fishing fleets from the other four Canadian provinces on the gulf. Thus, that year, men consumed twice as many fish from these waters as the belugas did. Even then, there would have been many left for other predators to feed on, since gulf waters can be much more productive than shown by the above figures. During the 1970s and 1980s, Québec landings were six times higher than in 1929, averaging 250 thousand tons of fish per year. The record clearly shows that humans can be far greedier than beluga whales.

The minister's tour was triumphant, with every public meeting an appropriate venue for announcing new schools and new roads and for making commitments for future visits. The trip ended at Blanc-Sablon, the easternmost community on the border with the British colony of Newfoundland. From there, it was only a short trip to now-famous Greenley Island for a commemoration of the landing of the *Bremen*. Minister Laferté climbed to the top of the lighthouse tower, from which he was shown a stone cairn with a bronze plaque in the middle of a concrete pond about one hundred feet square, which held the water supply that operated the motor of the foghorn. The minister could not but marvel at the good luck of the aeronauts who had managed to find a tiny flat surface of ice on this rocky island to absorb the shock of the landing, thus saving their lives. He looked south, trying to imagine over miles of water the restored *Bremen*, which now hung suspended high from the ceiling of Grand Central Station in New York. On that same day, President Hoover in Washington was congratulating yet another pioneer, Captain Eckener, who had just completed a tour around the world in a zeppelin. He was of the opinion that the future belonged to crafts lighter than air.

In September, as guest speaker at the monthly lunch of the Kiwanis Club in a gilded room of Château Frontenac, Cuisinier hailed the war against the whales as a great success. A second plane had arrived on the front, piloted by Lt. E. O. "Fizz" Champagne, another veteran of the Great War, who proudly wore his Distinguished Flying Cross. When a single bomb was dropped, five whales were found dead, which, according to Cuisinier, accounted for a small percentage of the total kill. Overall, after a mere fifteen to twenty bombs had been launched, Cuisinier claimed that the belugas were terrorized and that fishing was back to its normal high catches. Conversely, at the close of a one-week truce, the cod had disappeared again.

The ministry's assessment of the war was at variance with Cuisinier's. Superintendant of Fisheries Guibaut reported that there were fewer belugas but that cod were still mostly absent from the fishing grounds. The fighting had cost the ministry $29,680.91—

or about 21 percent of its entire budget for maritime fisheries, and
had been criticized by opposition members of the legislature. An
unsigned departmental memo acknowledged that although many
things had been learned from the summer's efforts, better results
could have been expected. It suggested that, in spite of some
improvement to the fishery, the policy for the coming year be
reevaluated. Plainly, this meant that the bombing of whales had
been judged unprofitable, although no statistics were ever produced
on the final tally. Bombings were not resumed the following year,
and Cuisinier would later say that what had been most lacking in
this adventure was perseverance.

This the minister did not lack, for he wrote in the introduc-
tory section to his "General Report of the Minister of Colonization, Mines and Fisheries of the Province of Québec " for 1929–30:

*Unfortunately, the maritime fisheries were not as productive as
expected in some areas of the North Shore, although market prices were
much higher than usual. The meagre success of the fisheries must be
attributed to the presence of the beluga whales. As an answer to the
fishermen's wishes and in order to improve on the fishery, my department waged war on the beluga. We did not merely commission boats
with gunmen to hunt down the whales, but even bombed them from
the air. Through such means and others that still have to be tested,
will we succeed in eradicating them from the St. Lawrence and thus
bring our fisheries back to their previous productivity? Only the future
can tell.*

The new strategy was announced the following year. Instead
of paying regular wages to gunmen, the ministry now promised
to pay fifteen dollars for every pair of beluga flukes handed in to
one of its officers. This generated much bustle among fishermen,
and Father Garnier was presumably still very active as well, since

he received his regular bonuses for the next few years. For professionals who operated weirs or hunted belugas from boats, like Joseph Lizotte of Rivière-Ouelle, the bounty was an additional incentive. Mere flukes had suddenly become worth as much as the skin and the rendered blubber of the belugas.

After eight years of bounties, the ministry carried out its first-ever biological study on the whereabouts and the feeding habits of the beluga whale in the St. Lawrence. Doctor Vladykov and his assistants set up camp on a beach to examine the stomach contents of animals shot offshore. In more than one hundred stomachs, they found one salmon and some cod but mostly prey of no local commercial value, such as sand lance, capelin, sculpins, clam worms, small clams, squid, octopus, and assorted crustaceans. Vladykov's report to the minister concluded that there was no relationship between the apparent abundance of the whales and the success of the fisheries. It recommended that the bounty be terminated, a measure that was adopted early in the summer of 1939. By then, bounties had been paid on a total of 2,499 beluga whales, whose useless flukes were buried or burned, their bodies left to rot on the beach or set adrift in the Gulf of St. Lawrence. Thus ended a deliberate and concerted effort at eradicating a cetacean population, an attempt like none other ever carried out in North America.

The cancellation of the bounty, which coincided with the war that Hitler was about to inflict upon the world, reduced the toll on beluga sharply. The river again belonged to the commercial fishermen who had been active exploiting the beluga since the early days of the colony in the 1600s. There are no statistics for the first two centuries of this fishery, but between 1866 and 1930, the year before the bounty was instituted, it has been estimated that an average of 185 belugas were landed every year (with a high of nine hundred in 1915). The bounty episode raised the annual toll to 366 animals. From 1939 to 1953, only some eighty-three belugas found their way to the market annually (with a high of 403 in 1942). It is not clear whether this decreased return was due to a drastic reduction in the number of whales remaining in the river or to the obsolescence of whale products in a market radically transformed by postwar industrialization. Only scattered catches occurred through the 1960s and 1970s, including occasional kills by sports hunters and pot-shooters. In 1979, the species was given legal protection in the St. Lawrence.

⌒⟶

*T*he steady drone of our airplane engine was interrupted by a change in pitch of the propeller. I woke up to see our small craft headed for Murray Bay and the airfield beyond the hollow in the mountains where the village sits by the river. At the head of the bay rose the flume from a paper mill whose effluents were for a long time discharged directly into the river. Under us, the tide was low, exposing rocks on which some seals were resting. They were rather large, probably gray seals. Like belugas of old, this species had until recently been subjected to bounties, an easy scapegoat for appeasing fishermen over the dwindling of fish stocks. Today, the fish have gone completely again, and the gray seals, said to be more numerous than ever, are among those targeted for culling.

The dark conifer forest on the hills around the bay was strewn with yellow and red patches of deciduous trees. Fall came early to this northern land dotted with small pastures carved out of the forest and sprinkled with cows. The scenery reminded me of a farm farther east, where I had been some years before in November. Carrying the heavy case holding our sampling gear, Daniel

Lefebvre, Richard Plante, and I trudged through a pasture and down to a hidden cove where the carcass of a dead beluga had landed among the first ice floes of the season. It was a huge male, fourteen feet nine inches long and relatively fresh, but impossible to remove for a necropsy under the circumstances. After examining the carcass outside and inside and collecting the teeth and a blubber sample, we climbed to the farmer's house, where his wife invited us in to warm up. We sat in the kitchen overlooking the river, steel blue on that chilly day. The man seemed to be in his early sixties and, as I always did when meeting local people his age, I asked if he had ever hunted beluga whales. To my surprise, he said yes, once. Decades earlier, his brother and he had shot a whale just offshore. They had towed it to the cove and rendered the blubber on the beach. The oil had filled a forty-five-gallon steel drum that they had not sold that season because the only buyer had already made his annual run along the coast. In the end, he said, they never did sell it.

My heart pounded. Was there a possibility that this barrel was still available? As far as the farmer knew, it was still by the shore under a small tree. Within minutes, we were on our way, the farmer carrying a large wrench and me following with glass jars and a ladle from the kitchen. He took us to a small stand of stunted black spruce trees half grown over by bushes and tall, withered weeds. It was here, said the farmer. As we walked into the thicket and parted the lower branches, we saw an old drum leaning against the scrawny trunk of a tree that did not seem to have grown at all for thirty years. The steel drum was brown with rust built up in small flakes around the lip and over the screw cap on top. The farmer unscrewed it with suprisingly little effort, exposing black threads coated with a greasy substance. When he lifted this lid up, the unmistakable smell of beluga oil filled the hollow space within the grove.

I scooped up several jarfuls of the yellow-brown oil made viscous by the cold weather. Back at the farmhouse, I wanted to know more about this particular animal. All the farmer could recollect was that the whale was a white adult. But his wife, over a few cups of tea, recalled that she was a young bride when her brother-in-law had moved out of the region and was able to ascertain that the animal must have been killed between 1950 and 1955. As soon as I returned home, I sent the oil to the laboratories of my chemist colleagues Derek Muir and Ross Norstrom and waited anxiously for the results. They came back with a shock: the beluga's blubber contained eight parts per million (or eight milligrams per kilogram) of PCBs and twenty-nine parts per million of DDT. Since the whale had died in 1955 at the latest, contamination of the St. Lawrence ecosystem was already well under way four decades ago.

The first aluminum smelting operations were set up on the shore of the Saguenay in the late 1930s, initiating extensive contamination by polycyclic aromatic hydrocarbons (PAHs). From 1947 onward, a chemical plant in the same vicinity discharged tons of mercury into the river. At the same time, all around the St. Lawrence and Great Lakes basin, industrial and agricultural practices were making increasing use of various synthetic chemicals. PCBs were first used in 1929 for their insulating and heat-resisting properties, mostly in electrical transformers and condensers. The insecticide DDT was introduced to North America in 1946 and soon became widely used for pest control in intensive agriculture and forestry practices. For example, between 1951 and 1965, up to one million pounds of DDT were sprayed every single year over the forests of eastern Québec and New Brunswick to fight the spruce budworm. The blubber oil in the rusting barrel indicated that less than ten years after this insecticide had been introduced on the continent, some beluga whales in the still very rural and tranquil St.

Lawrence had already accumulated thirty parts per million of it in their blubber. So it was that, as the hunting of whales was becoming less intensive through the 1950s and 1960s, more insidious causes of death were in the making. Knowing the effect that these chemicals have on reproduction, perhaps we should not wonder why the large herds dwindled during that period.

In those days, DDT was also a household product. In the summer of 1954, Theodora Lizotte, sister of Marie-Simonne and daughter of Joseph, the beluga hunter, was not feeling well. She was now fifty-eight, a mother of nine children, and she still lived near Rivière-Ouelle, where the beluga weir fishery had been abandoned years before. Theodora had been ailing for a while when she heard of a neighbor taken to the hospital ill from exposure to a powdered insecticide. She now understood why she was sick herself, since she had used the same powder. In the spring, noticing tiny white moths feeding on her potted plants, Theodora had set them all in the bathtub and sprinkled the lot with DDT. Upon bending down to water the soil, she had inadvertently breathed a substantial amount of it. Thus, on the St. Lawrence, the progeny of both the hunters and the hunted were facing the same threats.

Our plane came to the edge of the single gravel strip of the small airfield. We stopped right by the oversize striped sock that hung limp on its pole. The wind had not increased here either, so both halves of the survey would therefore have been a complete success. The other team was waiting for us by the control building. We looked at each other as the two leaders exchanged a piece of paper. Their team had counted 229 belugas, ours 243. Total, 472. The population had not changed at all since we had started surveying six years before. The herd of beluga whales in the St. Lawrence was still a mere fraction of what it had been when the first plane flew over the river.

OPPOSITE PHOTO: Beluga Aydin, or Briz, who escaped from a military training facility in the Ukraine, begs for fish from sympathetic folks of Greze on the Turkish coast of the Black Sea. (PHOTO CREDIT: PIERRE BÉLAND)

Spy Hop

*T*he whale could still hear the battering waves that had been raging for hours, but its ears also picked up something different. Something missing. Among the various sounds pervading its pen, the whale could no longer pick up those that normally reverberated from a very conspicuous object. The animal moved forward from the calmer spot between two projections of the jetty, where it had been riding out the storm. It turned its melon head toward the open sea and sent several bursts of pulsed sound in that direction. Among the echoes returning in rapid succession, those that usually returned from a very familiar feature were absent.

They were the sound waves that usually reflected from the fence enclosing the whale in its pen. That signature sound should have been clearly audible to the whale, even through the fractured noises made by the mass of water mixing violently with air and smashing against the concrete walls. Puzzled, the whale scanned a wider area at various distances ahead. Almost immediately, it received an echo from a large piece of the fence lying conspicuously on the bottom of the bay. There were also some echoes with the proper signature returning from pieces of the fence that still hung from the walls on either side of the pen. But the main body of the netting was gone, leaving a gaping hole between the captive animal and the open sea.

The beluga whale hardly moved for hours while the wind calmed and the storm moved away. The situation was confusing for the trained whale. Normally, only a gate on the right side of the fence would be open to let him out. Usually there would also be loud noise from the boat that always accompanied the whale out into the bay for a training bout. The beluga's stomach started to churn, yearning for the fish handed him after each performance. But nothing more happened. In a way, that was not unexpected: the boat and the trainer never showed up when the weather was rough and the only pleasant and safe volume of water was under the waves, away from the surface and the hand that fed. The beluga went on scanning for a while before it made up its mind to move discreetly toward the shreds of net on the bottom. Their edges did not match those of the portal when it was pulled aside and the whale was taken out into the harbor to look for objects among the ships. The door was open, but not in a normal way. And the trainer was still not there. This was all very unsettling.

Then, carefully staying close to the bottom, the beluga swam through the large opening. In an instant, he was out of his pen and into the small bay next to the main harbor. Riding unseen many feet below the churning surface, he went silently past a long jetty, gently rubbing his belly against familiar pebbles. Veering left, he turned on his side as usual to beam a burst of sound that reverberated agreeably against a set of rusted forty-five-gallon drums half buried in the mud of the main channel. The whale then went straight for the first buoy, checking under it for a rounded object, which he would normally retrieve. There was nothing there tonight. Veering right, he entered the first docking basin, inside of which the noise from the waves faded considerably. From previous experience in this part of the harbor, the whale knew not to let his eyes touch and be stung by the polluted surface film. He barely surfaced, took a deep gulp of air, and dove in again, heading straight for the hull of the first submarine in the row. This time, he was going to get an object and obtain his reward.

There was the familiar noise of a flow of water coming from a depression near the stern of the submarine, which the whale knew would feel warm in his open mouth. Passing through this bubble of heated water, the whale swam all along the steel hull of the submarine, his sonar checking for any bulging object. At the bow, he scanned for more rounded objects inside each of the eight long hollows that opened into the hull like long inverted tubes. There was nothing there, either. He then swam on to the next hull, repeating the same procedure. But still there was nothing. Puzzled, the beluga surfaced. He was ready for a reward and awaited further instructions, but there were no fish to be had and his trainer was not there. For a while, he just floated vertically in the harbor, his head like a pure white cone over the black water, iridescent with oil slicks in the moonlight. On the other side of the basin, a sailor on his night watch looked absentmindedly from the deck of a minesweeper at this white thing that had just popped up. He thought it looked like a child's balloon discarded in the middle of a fleet of nuclear submarines.

In the morning, Professor Lev Mukhametov and marine mammal specialist Boris Zhurid toured the port of Sebastopol on the Ukrainian Black Sea, looking for the two whales that had escaped during the night. The Russians were confident that Igor, the younger of the two belugas, would turn up within a day or two, but somehow they sensed that Briz was gone for a long ride and might never be seen again. They thoroughly searched every docking basin, cruising around the scores of submarines and other warships of the Black Sea Marine Command of the former unified Soviet Navy. Here and there, they stopped to inquire about the whales from among the swarms of indolent and unkempt sailors who just lay about on deck as they had done too often since the dismembering of the union. Most of the men were Ukrainians, and they had not seen anything unusual. At noon, the crew of the whale training boat from the Biotechnical Systems Institute went back empty-handed to its berth, tying up next to the beluga pen, which had been ravaged by the storm. Thankfully, the other basins, containing dozens of dolphins and sea lions, had not been damaged.

⌐⟩

A few months later, the phone rang in my office on the first floor of an old stone house in downtown Montréal, Canada. It was a call from Amsterdam. From the other side of the Atlantic, Ann Dingwall of Greenpeace told me a story I could not quite believe. A beluga whale had been sighted on the Turkish coast of the Black Sea. No, I said, belugas are absolutely not native to that inland body of water. I suggested that the wild beluga population nearest to Istanbul was that of Spitzbergen or perhaps Greenland, over 3,500 miles away. For that matter, why not a beluga from the St. Lawrence? I thought, looking out through the window at the skaters on the iced-over pond in Lafontaine Park across the street. A mother firmly held both hands of her young daughter, who was obviously too naive a skater to understand the difference between walking and gliding.

Oh! The whale seemed to be fond of people and liked to be hand-fed? No, I told her, belugas do not normally behave that way in the wild. Certainly, it was logical to assume it was an escapee from some aquarium. Yes, the whale could possibly have come from a Soviet facility in the Crimea. From what Ann was telling me, I gathered that the Turkish Ministry of Environment would welcome my expertise. Large snowflakes had started to fall, blurring the view of the park, where the little girl now sat alone on the snowbank, watching her mother spin in a long coat like a dervish.

Only when I had hung up did I truly realize what I had gotten myself into. There was a beluga whale hanging around a couple of villages on the Turkish side of the Black Sea, where it had become a kind of local attraction. Ann had referred to unclear messages from the Ukraine suggesting that it had escaped from a facility in the Crimea the previous fall. Although the whale did not seem to be in any kind of need, several animal protection groups in Europe were campaigning to return it to its natural environment. But where exactly was the natural habitat of this particular whale? Where had it been captured? I had just agreed to inform the Turkish government on the health status of the whale and to make recommendations about how best to deal with the situation. That meant I had to fly to Turkey, which I had agreed to do before the end of the week. I dialed the number of Sylvain De Guise on the east side of town, knowing that, he, too, would be ready to go. It was Tuesday, March 3, 1992, and a snowstorm seemed about to engulf Montréal.

On Friday, the outside temperature was minus sixty-five Fahrenheit as the two marine mammalogists sped along at more than five hundred miles an hour, thirty thousand feet above the Atlantic. Upon boarding the Lufthansa jumbo jet, De Guise and I were quite confident that we would find the whale, check it out, and be back home shortly. Presently, Sylvain dozed off, his mouth wide open, and I began having second thoughts. I brooded over the odds of finding the whale in the world's largest inland body of water, twice the size of our five Great Lakes combined. It might elude us for days, and I could not afford to spend weeks away from my work. This was the off-season, when the St. Lawrence shore was iced over and we could not get to the live whales, while the dead ones could not drift to us. It was also the time when I went through the annual trial of finding the funds needed to study our own threatened belugas. Obviously, much was being spent by Europeans on this single animal in the Black Sea who, according to all reports, appeared to be in no immediate danger.

Here I was, still carrying my ghosts with me, haunted by the dead whales of the past years and those that would start coming in April after the ice was gone. This was my chance to touch a live beluga in the sea. I wondered if the whale, probably originating from somewhere in the Arctic, would look very different from our own belugas in the St. Lawrence. Leafing through my *Nelles Guide to Turkey*, I experienced a cultural preshock, awed by the number and persistence of successive conquerers who had trod over that part of the earth, hoping to carve a home out of the remains of previous civilizations. Opening the miniature Turkish dictionary I had purchased in Montréal, I realized that the modern Turkish alphabet was the same as mine. I might not understand anything, but at least I might be able to read and say some words. Whale=*balina,* white=*beyaz,* said the doll-size lexicon. *"Bay-yaz ba-lee-na,"* I uttered, pondering over the Russian equivalent for a white whale. For Russia was unmistakably looming in the background. This was not a straightforward case of examining a dead whale beached on the south shore of the St. Lawrence. This time, the opposite shore would be in a different country whose motives might not be benign.

Whether the whale had come from a republic of the recently dismantled Soviet Union or, less likely, from Rumania or Bulgaria—the only other countries bordering the Black Sea—it could only be a communist whale. Moreover, the whale was apparently in good condition, as evidenced by its playful behavior after months of wandering across the Black Sea. Therefore, like anything else that seemed to work in the former Soviet Union, I guessed that the beluga must have been military. Since the United States Navy held beluga whales in captivity for undisclosed purposes, the Russian Navy probably did the same. This meant that two whale experts from Canada, a NATO country just like Turkey, could be drawn into a diplomatic incident with the Warsaw Pact over a spying whale.

⌒

*M*eanwhile, across the world, a fax machine sputtered out a page in a secretarial room at the Naval Ocean Systems Center in San Diego, California. The United States Navy officer on duty picked it up, looked at the addressee's name, and checked his watch. It was dinnertime, but knowing the scientist would be at work, the officer phoned him. A moment later, Wayne Turl walked in, picked up the single sheet of paper, and walked back to his office without a word. What he had in hand was a partial copy, slightly blurred, of a page from the Turkish newspaper *Djumhureyet*. It featured a somewhat washed-out photo of a whale next to a rowboat, framed by a few columns of text, all totally undecipherable. Turl could make out only the words BEYAZ BALINA in the boldface headline. At the bottom of the page, under the printed text, there was a handwritten note in English that Turl understood readily: "V says you are alone."

Turl picked up the phone and dialed a number in Kailua, Hawaii. He heard his correspondent laugh at Turl's own dismay over the impossible Turkish language. He was told that the whale photo had come in with a transmission from an undercover contact in the Ukraine who had confirmed that the Russian Navy had actually *lost* the whale during some kind of storm back in November. The pen had been damaged and two of the whales had left on their own. Now that the Turkish government had every animal lover in Europe on its back, the Russians were neither admitting nor denying anything. They were simply saying that they were missing two whales that had been housed in an oceanarium for purely scientific objectives.

Turl hung up. He had never been sure if the Russians were using belugas for the same purpose as his. In any case they certainly were not doing so at present. With the Russian economy as it was and the problems with the Ukraine, they would not be working with whales for a while, even if they got their animals back. Turl looked at the Pacific Ocean. Down by the jetty, three belugas were making rounds in their pen, calmly puffing in the cool air. He loved working with these animals, who were so easygoing compared with the dolphins he had studied before. He stood by his desk, pondering the research project he had now been working on for years. At least for a while, he was relieved from the pressure of beating the Rus-

sians to the finish line, but that did not really put him any closer
to understanding how to design a system that would produce a very
narrow and directional beam of sound.

⌒

When, on the following night, Lufthansa flight 3834 from Frank-
furt landed in Ankara an hour late, De Guise said he felt like a
whale that had been beached for hours and told me that I looked
like one. The airport bus wound down an endless dark ravine
whose banks were dotted with a myriad of small lights, each one
marking the spot where a low-lying house would stand in the
morning. Their combined effect was that of a drive down the Milky
Way. Presently, the route was taken over by a roaring fleet of heavy
trucks and buses of all sizes hurtling down to the town or climbing away from it, more often than not on the wrong side of the
road, while minute cars whizzed by in either direction through
every gap. We got off in the middle of town against the backdrop
of a colossal mosque on higher ground. Its long, slender minarets,
flooded in artificial light, made it look like a giant landing mod-
ule ready to zoom back into space. We had selected this stop
because most passengers were getting out of the bus but regretted
our choice when we found ourselves drifting aimlessly in the middle of a live display of the varied ethnic groups and trades of the
country. No one paid any attention to us except a cab driver, who
came out of the diesel-fume smog to scoop us off the curb against
which we had been wedged by the crowd like two air bubbles.

The cab immediately rushed back into traffic, like all Turkish
cars evidently carrying a positive electric charge that prevented it
from bumping into others. We were taken to our hotel within a
mathematically impossible number of minutes, considering the

density of matter traveling along the city lanes. Unfortunately, it turned out that we had started from the wrong end of town, for the driver dropped us on the side of the four-lane boulevard opposite to where the hotel stood. Exhaustion overtook me, and I felt the elusive whale move farther away as we dragged our heavy suitcases onto this foreign shore where we had stranded.

Inside the hotel, we walked straight into a dimly lit dining room and ordered whatever people ate in Turkey at 10 P.M. with cups of the national drink, tea—*chay*, according to my dictionary. Eating alone at a large table was a guest who looked like Albert Einstein, wearing a khaki army jacket and behaving conspicuously as though he did not want to be noticed. We were soon joined by a short young man whose head was shaved. He introduced himself as Fabrizio Fabbri from Greenpeace in Rome. He announced that he had made all arrangements with the hotel, with the Ministry of Environment, and with a rental car agency so that we could drive to the Black Sea the next day. Upon hearing this, the man with the khaki jacket now behaved as if he wanted to be noticed. Fabbri introduced him as Emilio Nessi, a reporter with *Topolino*, an Italian Disney-owned children's magazine. Nessi wished to join the official party for the drive north to find the beluga whale. I agreed and, in my present muddled state of mind, thought how crafty the KGB could be!

Fabbri seemed to have everything under control, so De Guise and I went to bed at half past midnight, which was four in the afternoon and a full day later to us. I immediately sank into a deep sleep but woke suddenly in a panic, lying in the dark. I could hear through the slightly open window the sound of beating drums and a wail like that of a siren. Convinced that a war had started, I got up and walked to the large window, expecting to see a battalion marching down the main street. Three floors above a back street, a minaret with four loudspeakers called the faithful to the first prayer of the day. There was a lamp near the corner of the building, the sun was about to rise, but there was not a drummer in sight.

After breakfast, we went to the ministry. The senior staff already knew Fabbri and welcomed Sylvain and me in perfect French and English. They confirmed that the beluga whale was still around Sinop and Gerze, casually pointing to an area on a wall-size map as if everyone in the room had spent his childhood there. The ministry staff alluded to the fact that the figure 434 km written sideways between two pointers might be deceiving and that the drive almost due north would seem much longer. Would we be able to find our way among the Turkish language signs or would we rather have a guide accompany us? Based on our experience of the previous night, I thought a grand prix driver might come in handier, but Fabbri, who was still very much in control, said we would be fine.

Fabbri lived in Rome, so he did not even have to pay attention to the late-morning traffic as he drove our party of four out of Ankara. It was a good thing, since he kept his head turned toward the backseat most of the time, talking to us. We came out unscathed onto a country road filled with overburdened lorries and droves of buses full of people smoking cigarettes. For hours on end our red Tofas, the Turkish version of a Fiat, wound its way along the Anatolian plateau, which was apparently deserted of inhabitants for the winter. The landscape was biblical, with neatly tilled fields of dry soil and stones patchworked between barren hills and dry riverbeds. From time to time we saw a fortress built by the Franks during the last Crusade decaying on a rocky knoll. Scattered villages were tucked under groves of leafless trees; austere but well-tended mosques gave a stamp of permanency to assemblages of brick and stone houses. From a distance, they reminded me of

French Canadian villages along the St. Lawrence, clustered around their high-steepled churches.

There was no snow on the ground, but there was plenty in the distance covering a range of mountains that stretched like a wall against the horizon. Hours went by, the Italian babble in the front faded as Nessi fell asleep, and the French echo in the back disappeared when De Guise dozed off. And then, suddenly, the high peaks of the Ilgaz Range were no longer visible as the car ascended. The slope was steep, the air became crisp, and jumbled blocks of ploughed, icy snow lined the road. I inquired about Fabbri's experience with driving in the snow, and he reassured me with tales of crossing the Apennines behind Rome in winter. A few hundred yards ahead, there came the first patch of ice and snow over the road, and the car spun 180 degrees, like Hannibal on his first elephant trip over the Alps. The vehicle, now facing in the general direction of Africa, had to be driven back down toward solid ground before its driver was able to turn back uphill. The road ahead was iced over for miles, and from there on, we progressed like a shell inhabited by four snails, brushing against snowbanks for fear of smashing into the usual traffic of oncoming trucks and buses and an occasional alpine skier going downhill in the middle of the road.

In this icy landscape I felt I was in beluga country, and wondered if a whale going uphill would have picked up the skier on its sonar before the curve. We crossed the divide at the Ilgaz Pass, altitude 5,823 feet, and wound down through a forest and into a valley. There were still more than 120 miles to go, including another range, only slightly lower in altitude than the previous one. When we arrived at the second mountain pass two hours later, it was dark and snow had started to fall, which forced Fabbri to again inch his way up toward the pass at ten miles an hour. He tena-

ciously held onto the wheel in spite of numerous polite but somewhat insistent offers from both Canadians to relieve him. At this
point, I became convinced that our journey was not what it
appeared to be. It was but one step in our quest to save the St.
Lawrence beluga, an ordeal to strengthen our resolve, a glimpse
of what would occur if we failed and had to go looking for the
last beluga on earth.

Soon, the snow fell more thickly, and the car went even
slower. Unable to bear it a minute longer, I almost ordered the
driver to stop the car and to hand over the wheel. Fabbri, as if
awakened from a nightmare, gladly relinquished the wheel, and
both Italians retreated to the backseat, while the Canadians took
charge in the front. I jumped into the driver's seat and immediately sped away with sonar at full blast through flying
snowflakes as big as jellyfish.

⤙⟶

Wayne Turl was almost through eating his lunch, still sitting at
his desk, when the printer on his left started to hum. The com-
puter had finished running the simulation he had requested, and
the printing of the full results would take over fifteen minutes. Turl
finished his sandwich, stretched, and walked to the window on
the bay. It was a beautiful spring day in California, and the sun
shining on the water sent flashes of dull white off the backs of two
beluga whales swimming out to sea. They were playfully cavorting on either side of a small research boat that glided over the bay.
Turl smiled, wondering what Sam Ridgway was up to this time
and whether the whales would prefer playing or working today.

In the distance, Turl could see the outline of the floating pen
where beluga echolocation studies were carried out. It was while

he stood on the floating platform of a similar pen in which a trained beluga idly swam that the scientist had had his first hunch about the project his printer was now reporting on. He had sold his idea to his employer, the U.S. Navy, submarine warfare division. To them, sound was everything. Hiding your own craft and remaining silent while being able to detect other ships, yet discriminating between friend and foe, could make the difference between victory and defeat, between life and death. Like his colleagues, Turl had studied sea animals that survived by using sounds, initially working with dolphins and then discovering belugas. One day, while experimenting with one of them, he had become convinced that the animal was producing a particular quality of sound wave that could become of immense use in submarine warfare.

At first, he thought it would be simple to learn how the whales did it and then to transfer this knowledge into a usable technology. But the goal had proven elusive, and today, looking at the belugas in the bay, Turl decided to go back to the basics and retrace every single step of his research program. Perhaps, he thought, he would get another insight that would allow him a badly needed breakthrough. He went to a bookcase on his right, grabbed three heavy blue binders, and sat back at his desk, oblivious to the printer still buzzing figures away.

The first binder was labeled TARGET DETECTION, and the researcher leafed through it, stopping here and there. The various reports demonstrated that belugas are extraordinarily adaptive acoustic animals. Like dolphins, they use a natural sonar system to "see" objects in the water without using their eyes. They do this by producing sounds that travel like waves ahead of them and hit any objects in their paths. Part of the waves twist around the objects and disappear into the water ahead, but the main body of the waves returns to the whale as echoes from the objects. These echoes are received and analyzed by the whale's brain in order to give it information on the shape, size, and density of each object. The studies showed that belugas can do this even in the presence of noise from other sources. They detect targets by varying the types of sounds they themselves emit in order to override the background noise. Turl looked up from his binder and gazed at the glare on the bay: what the belugas did with sound was similar to what he himself did with light. His own eyes could adapt to confusing light and still make out individual objects against a bright background.

Another study in the binder showed that, unlike humans relying on vision, belugas can "see" objects that are hidden behind a screen. The whales achieve this feat by bouncing sound against the bottom of the sea or against the surface of the water. They thus receive echoes from targets situated on the other side of larger objects or lying beyond a noisy area through which their emitted sounds do not travel well. Altogether, the studies were clear on another point: belugas are far superior to dolphins in target detection under various conditions in their environment. Undoubtedly, belugas live in a more complex environment than dolphins, and they have evolved tools that may make the difference between life and death. In the Arctic, under a cover of ice, a whale still has to surface to breathe. It must find leads between ever-moving ice floes, even when these are a long distance away, and in the presence of intervening blocks of ice. Perhaps the belugas' more powerful tools also explain why they are less jittery than dolphins when presented with a novel situation and why they are easier to train for a variety of tasks.

The second binder was labeled SONOBEAM. Its first section contained a diagram of Turl's initial study on the propagation of bel-

uga echolocation signals. For this experiment he had used an eleven-
year-old male beluga, a Canadian whale captured at Churchill on
Hudson Bay. The whale had gone to the Kailua Laboratory in
Hawaii along with Turl, and they were both uncomfortable with
the heat. The diagram showed a corral with a floating divider that
held a hoop down into the water. In front of the hoop, at a depth
of about three feet, was a horizontal bar. The trial began when the
beluga extended its head through the hoop and bit the bar, indicating its readiness to perform. Then, a three-inch, waterfilled stainless steel sphere was lowered into the water about 260 feet in front
of the hoop, and the animal was cued to echolocate. Throughout
the trial, an array of underwater microphones re-corded every sound
produced by the whale. After completing its sonar search, the beluga backed out of the hoop and reported on the presence or absence
of the sphere by striking one of two response paddles.

When Turl analyzed the recordings, he knew he was onto something. Like those of dolphins, the sounds produced by the beluga
were not standard waves that traveled in all directions, like rip-
ples on the water where a stone has been dropped. Instead, the
beluga's sound progressed forward within a relatively narrow path,
both horizontally and vertically. Such a pattern of sound had been
observed before in bottle-nosed dolphins, but the beluga's path was
much narrower. Most of the sound emitted by the beluga to locate
the sphere moved ahead as a single cone within an angle of only
five degrees relative to the mouth of the whale, like a person speaking into a gigantic underwater megaphone. Turl reasoned that the
narrower and more directional beam of sound produced by the
beluga was due in part to its larger head and in part to its highly
mobile melon. He had observed how a beluga could modify the
profile of its melon at will, even altering it into the shape of a
cupola very similar to a small satellite dish.

Author with twelve-year-old adult female found adrift on the St. Lawrence near Tadoussac in July, 1993. She was bearing a term fetus, but her mammary glands were atrophied and would not have produced any milk. The cause of death could not be determined.

A pod of belugas cavorting in St. Marguerite Bay, in the Saguenay Fjord, thirty miles from its confluence with the St. Lawrence. Such rare behaviors as surfing and swimming with heads held high occur more often in this small bay where groups of whales spend up to a few days at a time.

Pascolio, a hunchback, is a young beluga whale who, as a juvenile, was very inquisitive and regularly swam to the research boat. As he approached sexual maturity, he seemed to lose interest in humans.

Pascolio liked to investigate underwater cameras and other objects dropped in the water.

The beluga in the forefront is Domino, one of a group of juveniles whom the research team has known almost since their births. Domino has replaced Pascolio as the research team's darling. Here, he is introducing us to one of his friends.

An adult male carcass drifted onto the south shore of the St. Lawrence in August, 1988, one of twenty-one dead belugas found that year. An autopsy revealed a peritonitis, necrosis of a testicle, mouth ulcers, and severe inflammation of the gums. The bulging and furrowed thoracic area shows that this 20-year-old animal was quite emaciated.

Éliane, younger daughter of the author, on the look-out for belugas during a week-long study trip on the St. Lawrence estuary.

Skipper Daniel Lefebvre attempts to determine the sex of the individuals in this pod, while photographer Flip Nicklin looks on. Belugas readily come to investigate the researchers who try to unravel the secrets of the whales' lives in the St. Lawrence river.

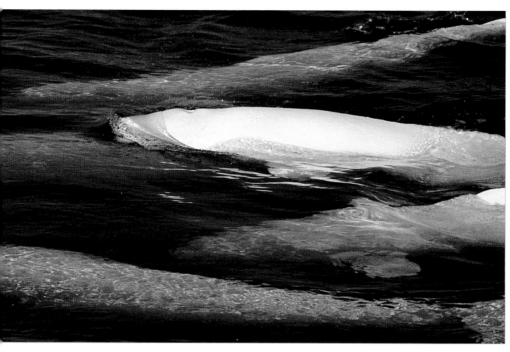

pod of belugas passes without investigating the boat, the whales swimming toward a goal known only to them.

tiny beluga calf lying momentarily listless on the back of an adult, minutes after being born on the St. Lawrence. number of adults hug close together, assisting mother and calf during this precious and never before photo-aphed event.

Veterinary pathologist Dr. Daniel Martineau tending to premature female calf found abandoned in the St Lawrence. After four days in captivity, it died of suffocation due to malformation of the respiratory tract.

Veterinary pathologist Dr. Sylvain De Guise holding a baby beluga while Dr. Janie Giard inserts a tube fo force-feeding. This newborn male was found abandoned in the St. Lawrence and kept alive for ten days befor it died of respiratory problems.

The beluga whale Aydin (also known as Briz or Palla di Neve) being fed by fans off the village of Greze on the Turkish Black Sea. This animal escaped from a military facility in the Ukraine during a storm in 1991. After being recaptured, he escaped again, and is still roaming the Black Sea.

Very unusual in a young adult male, Aydin's teeth are completely worn down, suggesting they were intentionally filed for some undisclosed purpose.

Aydin, showing the scar on his upper right lip.

Pierre Béland

photographer unknown

Beluga whale at rest vertically underwater, calmly observing the research boat and photographer. Well-rounded forms and folds on the belly evidence the thick layer of blubber typical of the species.

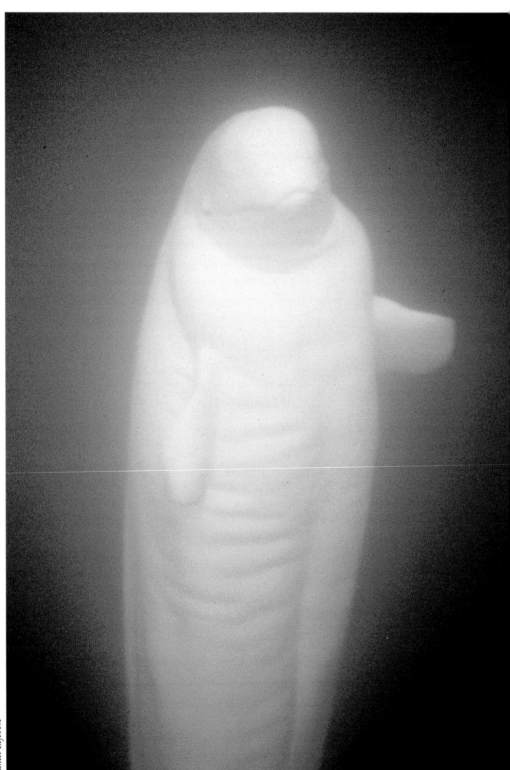

At the time, the researcher had reasoned that a larger and more focused apparatus might produce an even narrower beam— one that could be aimed at a particular spot in the ocean where only friendly ears would hear. This beam could not be detected in any other direction, and the emitter of this sound would therefore not give away its position to the enemy. This would be the ideal tool for exchanging information between friendly submarines or for transmitting data between a submarine and an underwater relay station with a link to the surface and from there onward to headquarters.

The third binder Turl did not need to open: he knew it by heart. It was a collection of papers, notes, and reports, many of them still bearing the word CLASSIFIED. They were the numerous contributions from several navy labs that had led to a great technical achievement, a search device installed on U.S. nuclear submarines. The binder bore the name SONARRAY.

⌐⟶

*T*he drive down the mountains went as smoothly as a toboggan ride, and we entered Sinop by the sea at close to midnight in a drizzle. After some searching, we found our hotel on the Black Sea—a drowsy stone building dripping under a rainy wind from the north. Its darkened entrance faced the old city walls, whose condition under the yellow streetlight suggested they had last been repaired under Mithridates, king of the Pontus, in 100 B.C.

The crenellated fortifications proved much sturdier when Sylvain and I climbed them in the morning. From up there, the *Euxeinos Pontos*, as Plutarch called the Black Sea in his chronicle of the adventures of Alexander the Great, was totally uninviting, with heavy clouds and whitecaps everywhere. There was not a whale in sight, and a search out at sea for the beluga in such weather would have been futile. The leeward parapet looked out on a smelly basin that held a cluster of small fishing rowboats the shape of tubs, closely guarded by a battalion of grebes and their cormorant officers. The windward rampart led to a bastion where a tribe of young boys were flying large hexagonal kites. Their crafts were made of translucent strips cut from steel-blue and green plastic bags, wrapped over a six-armed wooden cross and joined together by pieces of black electrical tape. One kid had hopelessly entangled the nylon lead to his craft when it had fallen flat into the black water below. De Guise helped him retrieve it, and thus was the morning not totally wasted.

Beyond the bastion, the main harbor was clogged by a fleet of modern fishing vessels, all apparently decommissioned for the season. Nearby, we walked by a row of red-and-white plastic pails holding neatly rolled nylon gill nets made of translucent green monofilament. They were lined up against a pale yellow and rather soiled building, under one of its large four-paned windows. Behind the glass, four old men wearing fur hats were playing cards on a red-carpeted table while two others stood behind, looking at us with Delphic smiles. It was Monday, but we sensed we had happened onto some kind of holiday in this fishermen's town, a town probably not likely to welcome a beluga, who would be cursed, like all of his kin, as a fish gobbler and a destroyer of fishing gear.

We ambled toward the downtown area on the other side of the sea wall and its array of Greek, Roman, Byzantine, and Turkish dwellings built from whatever materials happened to fall off the fortifications over the centuries. We went through a busy tangle of sooty streets and alleys where stray cats searched around ocher stucco houses from which lilac-and-white sheets hung to dry in the wind. There, beyond a grove of romantically decayed wooden houses of late Ottoman architecture, we had our first glimpses of the beluga.

Every other shop in the center of town had a photo of the whale. It could be seen from above on the door of a bakery, poking its big, rounded white ball of a head next to that of a diver in a black rubber suit. On the next block, in the window of a shoe store, three men were standing in a rowboat on a glossy bay whose sheen was frosted here and there by wisps of wind. The sun shone equally on the bow of the boat and on the melon of the beluga against a backdrop of mountains dappled with snow. The men had dark mustaches, dark hair, and dark eyes, and looked strong and hardened by work and weather, fearless and proud, yet one of them was holding an orange-brown water polo ball, which he was about to throw to the whale. Behind the counter of a café around the corner, the gaping mouth of the beluga could just grasp the water polo ball, and the Black Sea sparkled through the open space between the ball and the corner of the wide-open jaws. Under the picture, the word *Aydin* was written in bold letters.

In the street market, we were greeted by very healthy-looking mackerels glistening in the rain, neatly piled next to a sprawl of sardines on a wooden stall. For the next few blocks, every kind of vegetable, fruit, and nut could be seen, huddling under makeshift awnings tended by friendly human faces. De Guise bought some dried apricots that looked like warm suns in an otherwise gloomy day, and I settled on *eckmeck*, in the form of a thick and crusty rounded loaf. Soon we arrived at the wall on the other side of town and, climbing it, discovered that Sinop had been built on a peninsula.

There we ate the bread and fruit, hugging the stones to hide from the bitter wind, thoroughly thrilled to be here together and to have found the beluga. Some close-up photos of its head showed a large scar on the right side of the corner of the mouth, as if the whale had bitten into something that had gouged a big crescent-shaped chunk out of its upper lip. A number of snapshots of the wide-open mouth without a water polo ball showed completely worn-down teeth, a quite unexpected condition in an animal who otherwise looked like a rather young adult. The entry under *Aydin* in the dictionary was "bright, clear."

⌇

*I*n Sebastopol that same morning, at the tip of the Crimean Peninsula on the north side of the Black Sea, the weather was cold, but the sea near shore was calm. At the Biotechnical Systems Institute overlooking Kazachia Bay, Professor Mukhametov was satisfied with the exchanges he had had with his colleagues in Sebastopol and St. Petersburg. Vladimir Akhutin and Yuriy Rybalchenko had agreed to a text that would be distributed abroad regarding Briz, the beluga whale that the Turkish press was calling Aydin. Incredibly, the naval press officer in Moscow, Novikov, had also swiftly approved it.

The professor went to the communications center to have the text transmitted immediately to Ankara, Amsterdam, and a number of other European cities that had sent pressing requests for information. The message was laconic; its main body was merely an identification sheet collated from the whale's file. The letter sent to Ankara contained in addition a clear statement of ownership, along with an intent to repossess the beluga whale.

THE VETERINARIAN REPORT FOR SEA ANIMALS

Briz
town Vladivostok   Oceanarium TINRO

DATA OF SEA ANIMAL

Species	Beluga (Delphinapterus Leucas)
Name	Briz
Sex	Male
Age	Born in 1984
Special marks	Scar on the upper and lower lip on the left side
Date of capture	3rd May 1987
Place of capture	Island Bajdukova in Sakhalin's Bay in Okhotsk Sea
Transportation	By the helicopter MI-8 (24.07.87) to the base "Vitjaz"
Delivery to dolphinarium:	September 1987 by helicopter from base "Vitjaz"

Transferred to Sebastopol oceanarium, May 1991

MEASUREMENTS CHARACTERISTICS	UNIT	DATE: 9th August 1991
Length	cm	400.0
Weight	kg	850.0
Condition of eyes		good
Condition of hearing		good
Condition of teeth		sufficient
Breathing frequency	per min.	3,5
Jumping, activity		active

Escaped from oceanarium, September 1991

⌒⟶

*L*ater that day, Gulshen Kugu, a representative of the Ministry of Environment of Turkey, arrived in Sinop to act as liaison. She settled us at a government guest house near the main harbor, where she showed us a copy of the beluga ID card as received from Russia. It confirmed what many had suspected—the escapee from the Soviet Union had originally been captured off Siberia. The whale appeared to have at least some link with the military, since its first holding facility had been a military base in Vladivostok, Siberia. How—certainly by air and not on the TransSiberian railroad—and why it was moved to the Crimea was, however, not alluded to. Interestingly, the presumed year of birth of the beluga, 1984, meant that it was barely eight years old, which made it a recently matured male, certainly not an old animal. Its pedigree had obviously been hastily translated from the Russian. For example, the photos seen in town indicated that the lip scar was on the right side, not the left; quantifying the condition of teeth as "sufficient" probably meant that the normal number of teeth were present. Back at the guest house that night, I mulled over the obvious discrepancy between the worn-out teeth and the age of the animal as I fell asleep, imagining the whale on a flight through six time zones, a distance almost exactly the same as that between Sinop and Montréal.

Again I awoke in a sudden panic in the dark, hearing through the closed window the sound of beating drums. This time I got up swiftly and went straight to the window, where I was met by the mouth of a loudspeaker bolted to the stone face of an old minaret, pointing directly at my nose. The electronic muezzin was silent, however, and the sound was coming from below. Down in the middle of the narrow street, three men were walking slowly, one of them clutching an old drum. The group went to the other side of the street and stopped at a door to beat the drum. I dressed, went out in the brisk air, and walked on the damp pavement in the direction the rattle appeared to have gone. There was a café nearby, brightly lit and drowned in cigarette smoke. It overflowed with male patrons sitting at small tables in front of rummy tiles and backgammon boards and wearing the most solemn of faces in the middle of the night. All along the street and on every other block, the restaurants and cafés were open and equally busy with customers sipping tea and eating pastries. The rumble of drums was still audible, fading away and resonating deeper within the stone maze of the old town. I could not interpret the bearing of the various echoes and went back to my room. It was just as well that I could not go back to sleep since in a short while the loudspeaker outside the window started blaring the plaintive recording of an ancestral muezzin voice.

At daybreak the wind was down and the sun shone between scattered clouds. We boarded the training vessel from the University of Sinop and sailed toward the small town of Gerze, some fifteen miles to the southwest. On the way, I told Gulshen Kugu about my adventure of the night. This was the month of the Ramadan, she said, when the faithful were forbidden to eat from sunrise to sunset. One hour or so before the call for the first prayer of the day, drummers walked around town to wake people up so that they could have a last bite before sunrise. Children were told it was customary to have a small offering ready, for they might otherwise be abducted from their homes.

Our boat arrived off Gerze and there we found the beluga, who was behaving like the star whose photos were displayed all over Sinop. On the bay near the pier, small groups of men in wooden rowboats were competing with a diver in a black wetsuit for the attention of the beluga, which milled among them in the greenish blue water. Sylvain and I went down in a small inflatable raft to have a closer look at the animal. De Guise's veterinary examination, although cursory under the circumstances, indicated that it was in good condition, not thin, obviously in a playful mood, and without any obvious injury. When I dangled a fish above the open mouth of the whale, we clearly saw that its teeth were worn down to the gums, even more so farther in on the upper jaw, a pattern not at all like the usual wearing of beluga teeth in the wild. The worn-out faces of its teeth were not the color of ivory but brownish, more so at the center, although there was no visible inflammation or injury to the gums. A young man in the nearest boat held a water polo ball, ready to throw it to the whale as soon as the examination was over. It struck me for the first time that the whale would not have been able to grasp such a big ball if its teeth had extended into the mouth their normal length of an inch or so.

I stroked the whale's melon and pulled the fish higher. The beluga rose smoothly toward my hand, like a buoy losing its ballast. Swiftly, Sylvain brushed a swab against the inside lining of the whale's mouth to get a sample for bacteriological and genetic analyses. Immediately, the whale snapped and sank down with the fish. I leaned back against the soft side of the inflatable, glad that my worst fears had not materialized: the whale was real and we had found it. It was tamer than our own whales in the St. Lawrence but otherwise much the same. This mild winter morning at the edge of Asia was just like a cool summer day in my arctic oasis by the Saguenay fjord in Canada. For a moment, I felt at home, thoroughly delighted to be at last feeding one of my whales in the wild. Of course, it was unusual to be among black-mustached men on a fleet of small, tublike boats in white paint except for a broad red line around their freeboards and the letterings of their names on the bow.

I caught the dark eyes of a Turkish boy peering at me from the rowboat *Toto Kemal*. He seemed angry, and I imagined he had heard the rumor that we had been asked to check on the health of the whale before it was taken away. Like his father beside him, he wanted it to stay, now that they had a small business taking whale-watching journalists out on the bay. Today, their passenger was our friend Emilio Nessi, looking like a joyful and plump house mouse who had just found a piece of cheese. He was running from bow to stern, snapping pictures for his children's magazine. He had no experience with whales; when given this assignment by his editor some weeks before, he had thought that a beluga was a Russian sturgeon. He could not have known that this whale would change his life. It was *Amore a prima vista*, love at first sight! Nessi had given the beluga his own choice of a name, Palla di Neve—Snowball—and, like most animal-protection groups across Europe, he was asking the Turkish government to allow the animal to be taken to a facility where it would be rehabilitated for an eventual return to its natural environment.

Nessi was aware that Sylvain and I did not agree with this plan. We judged it costly and hazardous, if only because in its native Siberia the whale risked being shot at by humans who might not be as friendly as the beluga would expect. Here, on the contrary, where the beluga had been thriving on its own for months, its presence had started to inspire a change of attitude toward whales among local communities. In time, we hoped that the harried dolphins and porpoises native to the Black Sea might be spared by fishermen, if only for their tourism potential. Already, quite contrary to tradition, we had learned that the town of Gerze had adorned its coat of arms with a beluga whale!

⌒

A few days later, Sylvain and I were back in Montréal. The main recommendation in our report to the Turkish Government was to leave the whale where it was. Thus, although for different reasons, we agreed with Nessi and the local people on one issue: nobody wanted the beluga returned to its pen in the Ukraine. No one but the Russians who, secretly, were already on their way to the Turkish coast.

OPPOSITE PHOTO: **Briz and Igor, the Russian belugas, back in a pen at Laspi in the Crimea.** (PHOTO CREDIT: EMILIO NESSI)

In the Arena

On a warm morning in early April, a research vessel geared like a trawler and waving the Ukrainian flag anchored off Gerze on the Black Sea coast of Turkey. Lev Mukhametov stood on the bow, anxiously scanning the jade water with binoculars. For the last few days, he had been pursuing the beluga along the coast, never getting close enough to attempt to capture him. He searched across the bay, rimmed by the white town and the pink strokes of apricot trees in full blossom on the lower mountain slopes. Almost immediately, he saw the beluga whale swimming toward him, and he motioned to Boris Zhurid to come out from the wheelhouse.

Zhurid went down on deck, where the sailors were lifting a large net and an orange canvas stretcher with the boom. Zhurid and another trainer put on wetsuits and climbed into the net, which was then moved over the side and lowered to just above water level. A pail of fresh fish, caught overnight for the occasion, was handed down to the divers. In just a few minutes Briz swam alongside the ship and happily took the fish thrown at him. Slowly, the vessel sailed away from shore, the whale following, and stopped around the three-mile limit in international waters, as agreed upon with the Turkish government. There, the net and stretcher were lowered slightly below the surface, and the divers swam out to its edge, now holding the fish in their hands for the beluga to come closer. As soon as the whale was directly over the trap, the net was lifted slowly. Thus, in a matter of minutes, a beluga whale from Siberia was recaptured in the Black Sea and bound for the Crimea.

Some distance away, the Turkish man from Gerze and his son on the *Toto Kemal* were watching the event that they had dreaded. On board today was a reporter for Agence France Presse, who had arrived from Istanbul two days earlier. He took a last picture of the beluga as it naively took one more fish from the hand of a diver, its large white head poking down from the net in which the rest of its body was well ensnared. To the reporter, this marked the happy ending of a somewhat uncomfortable assignment. To the man from Gerze, it was a sad farewell to a whale that he had come to consider Turkish and that had brought more visitors to Gerze than ever before. To the boy, it was a fateful affair, a preordained ending: the drummer of the Ramadan had come, but there was no offering. The beluga had been abducted to a foreign land.

The following night, the Russian ship arrived at its destination on the other side of the Black Sea. Waiting under the dim light on the jetty was a trainer, Alla Azovtseva, relieved to see that Briz was puffing calmly. The whale was on the stern deck in just a few feet of water inside a makeshift pool made of plastified canvas supported by steel wires and barely long enough for him. Water spilled over one end of the pool when the ship touched the jetty at mooring, a hint of what would have happened had the ship hit rough weather on its fifteen-hour crossing. In a short while, the boom lifted the beluga in a stretcher, slid him over the ship's handrail, and deposited him on the rough tarmac on the side of the narrow jetty, which looked onto a large pen. A dozen men lifted the stretcher by hand and painstakingly moved the animal to the very edge. Then those on the waterside moved away while the others lifted their own end higher. The whale rolled and fell down several feet into the bay like a laundry bag. In a few seconds, the beluga was up at the surface, taking the fish that Alla handed him.

⌒→

*T*hat morning in Montréal, a thin hail caught me jogging in Lafontaine Park. It was April 7th. It should have been spring, but I returned home chilled to the bone and picked up my soggy copy of the morning paper *La Presse* by the door. Leafing through it over a cup of coffee, I saw an AFP photo of the torso and head of a beluga hanging down from a net, his snout touching the water. I had been back from Turkey for more than three weeks, unable to obtain any information on the whale. Now I read that he had joined the fifty or so members of his species that lived in captivity in various parts of the world. I worried for the animal, certain that veterinary care and humane conditions for captive animals were not on the list of priorities in the chaotic republics of the former Soviet Union. I had been to Russia ten years earlier, before *glastnost* and the present revolution, back when things were said to be normal. Yet long queues formed every day in front of food stores where fresh meat and fresh fish were particularly scarce or even unavailable outside the major cities. Not a good place for an aquatic carnivore, I now thought.

Outside, the hail turned into snow, wetting the kitchen window with heavy flakes that I wished would seal the fate of winter. Within a fortnight, the spring tide on the lower St. Lawrence would lift the shelf ice up and take it away to the sea, exposing the shoreline, freeing the harbors. We would be on the water again to see how many of our own belugas had returned from the gulf, knowing that the missing would turn up dead on the shore, not as tamed animals in a tank somewhere. Even if live captures had been allowed in the St. Lawrence, hardly anyone would have wanted to take a risk on such contaminated and unhealthy animals. This had not always been the case, though, and of all beluga populations, those from the St. Lawrence had the longest pedigree as captives. The song of the beluga has earned him the name sea canary, but those from the St. Lawrence also deserve to be called aquarium guinea pigs.

In 1861, P. T. Barnum, always in search of oddities for his American Museum in New York, heard of fishermen in the St. Lawrence who had caught a live white whale. He immediately began constructing a brick-and-cement tank, forty by eighteen feet, in the basement of his building. Then, going by rail to Rivière-Ouelle, he chartered a sloop to cross over to Île-aux-Coudres, where he contracted with a party of twenty-four fishermen. After several days, they succeeded in capturing two whales in the weir. The belugas were laid in wooden boxes lined with seaweeds for transport by rail to New York. Barnum left ahead of the whales and, in his usual wheeler-dealer way, asked telegraph operators at every station to inform their townspeople of any message about the whales that passed over the wire and to advertise the time at which they would be going by. The commotion along the seven hundred-mile line can well be imagined, culminating in a rush of thousands to see the whales swim in the basement tank in downtown Manhattan at Ann Street and Broadway. These two belugas from the St. Lawrence were the first cetaceans ever maintained in captivity.

The belugas died after a few days, which Barnum attributed to their being in freshwater and breathing foul air in the badly ventilated cellar, where no one knew how to properly care for and feed them. Undeterred, Barnum had a second tank built of slate and glass plates, twenty-four feet square, which he supplied with saltwater pumped from New York Bay and furnished with two more whales from the St. Lawrence. These also died within days but were as soon replaced by a fifth and sixth whale! One of them, a male of ten feet, became tame enough to be harnessed to a small car in which it drew a young lady around the tank. When Barnum's Museum burned down in 1865, two more live white whales that had just arrived from the St. Lawrence were in the glass aquarium. The fire had started in the room where a small engine pumped water for the tank; the whales burned to death and were still steaming when their owner arrived on the scene.

This limited success encouraged the live capture of another beluga in a seine net off the lower North Shore of the Gulf of St. Lawrence in the late summer of 1877. This one was bound for England, where it arrived after a long ordeal aboard ship, compared with brief flights on chartered jets on which belugas nowadays travel. The whale was put on board a sloop to Montréal, from which it traveled by railway to New York, a total journey of fourteen days. It was held in the aquarium reservoir at Coney Island until its departure on the German steamer *Oder* on September 15. A fair sum must have been paid for its capture and transport, since the owner had insured the animal with the Paris Marine Insurance Company for £500—undoubtedly the first underwriting of a whale.

In the meantime, at the Royal Aquarium in Westminster, a huge vat of wrought-iron plates was being riveted together. It was forty feet long, twenty feet wide, and six feet deep, rounded at the corners, its bottom covered in Portland cement. Holding 54,000 gallons of water, it was gigantic for the time, but well below the modern North American minimum acceptable standard of 95,000 gallons for a single beluga whale. When the ship arrived in Southampton on the twenty-seventh, the whale was transferred to the tender steamer, landed on the docks, and brought to London by the SouthWestern Railway on an open car, where it lay half embedded in seaweed, puffing in a large wooden box twelve feet in length.

Upon the beluga's arrival at the Aquarium, its keepers discovered that the water in its new tank was fouled because the cement had not set properly. While the whale waited four more hours in its box, the tank was emptied, the cement scraped off, and fresh water poured in. The beluga was finally slid into the tank, where it swam calmly after having traveled for thirty-seven days, most of the time out of water and without any food. It nevertheless disappointed many visitors because it simply breathed air instead of spouting water as whales were believed to do and because it was deemed too small for a whale. The beluga was a female about nine feet in length, which corresponds to a juvenile individual only three to five years old. If so, she should have been of a gray color, although witnesses reported her as creamy white. To sustain the beluga, live eels were placed in the tank, which the whale soon began to chase and capture. On the fourth day, following a brief period of listing and unequal breathing, the whale died, and the remaining eels immediately began to nibble at its fins. The autopsy, under the direction of Professors Flower and Garrod, diagnosed a pneumonia.

On May 27 of the following year, four more St. Lawrence belugas arrived at Liverpool on the Allan Line Steamer *Circassian*. Three appeared vigorous in their boxes, but one was dead, suffocated by the seaweeds when it turned over in its coffin during a lurch of the ship in rough weather. The survivors were to go into separate tanks in Manchester, Blackpool, and Westminster, but I do not know what became of them. In 1897, the New York Aquarium obtained two live belugas from Rivière-du-Loup—an adult female with an injury who lived five days, and an immature male who shed much skin and is said to have died choking on an eel twenty days after his arrival.

Many decades passed before live belugas were taken from the St. Lawrence River again. In 1962, the National Film Board of Canada subsidized the reconstruction of the weir trap at Île-aux-Coudres for the purpose of making a documentary film on that ancient tradition. Captured whales were not meant to be killed and rendered but to be sold live to oceanariums. The first successful catch was a young male who was sent to the New York Aquarium and displayed under the name *Blanchon*—the French Canadian name for a juvenile beluga in its fourth year. For a while, it shared a tank with Alex, a male beluga from Alaska, and later sired two calves, the first belugas ever conceived in captivity. Blanchon lived in New York for twenty years, quite an exception among St. Lawrence whales. Eight other animals brought to the New York Aquarium between 1963 and 1965, all under four years of age, died within six to eight months of their arrival. They were heavily parasitized with lungworms, perhaps a consequence of compromised immune systems, which would be consistent with the increasing flow of toxics in their natural environment at the time.

In 1964, a very young animal, said to have been only nine months old, was caught live in the weir at Île-aux-Coudres. It had, by prearrangement, already been sold to the Flamingo Park Zoo in Yorkshire, England. The beluga was taken by truck over the mountains to a Québec City suburb, where it was held for a week in a private swimming pool, sharing it with people who believed the whale enjoyed their company. Being so young, it had to be force-fed a mixture of herring and clams ground up with cream, fat, and vitamins. The whale was then set in a wet box for a trip by road to Montréal and put on board an Air France flight to Manchester, with a stopover in Gander, Newfoundland. I have been unable to find out what became of the beluga in its cramped, 26,400-gallon tank among exotic animals, but I suspect it would not have survived long.

The new weir at Île-aux-Coudres remained active through 1970. A total of twenty whales were caught and kept in a pond hastily dug out by the shore. Most whales died there while attempts were being made to sell them live to aquaria. This was during a period when very little was known about the status of the population in the river, a time that I consider to have been critical for its survival. In 1978, a Canadian government ministry granted a sum of about $84,000 to private interests toward the construction of a new weir for the purpose of creating jobs on the island. The grant was renewed in 1979 for an additional $100,000, with the added goal of stimulating tourism. Fortunately, the project never materialized because another ministry refused to issue a permit for catching belugas in the St. Lawrence: the population had just become protected by law.

I looked through the kitchen window at a thin magnolia in my yard trying to bloom this far north, its skinny branchlets covered in wet snow. I recalled the launching of our campaign, "Let's Adopt a Beluga." Shortly afterward, a friend had described to me the reaction of his young daughter when he had suggested they might adopt one. She had told her absentminded father that even though she loved the idea, they had to forego the opportunity since they did not have a swimming pool in their backyard.... Schoolchildren often write me about their own wishes for the St. Lawrence beluga. One of them is that the remaining whales should be taken into captivity temporarily until the river is cleaned up.

In the yard, the snow turned to rain and I thought about the people of Gerze, who had just lost their whale, and of what Emilio Nessi would tell his young readers has happened to the beluga in the Black Sea.

⤸

When Emilio Nessi saw a telex of the AFP photo in the mail slot of his Milan office, he believed his direst dream had become reality. The beluga was back in the military facility in Sebastopol, where, he had learned, the Russians had trained hundreds of dolphins and sea lions to protect the Soviet navy base in Kazachia Bay against intruders. The sea lions were drilled to find metallic objects and to locate small submersible equipment at sea. The dolphins were sentinels who, upon locating an intruder, pressed down one of two buttons on a console at the bottom of the bay, activating either a siren during the day or a bank of lights during the night. If needed, the dolphins would squeeze through special windows in the protective net, exiting into the open waters to investigate potential enemies. Like soldiers with bayonets, they were trained to attack and kill humans with the pointed steel helmets they wore on their rostrums.

Nessi had not found any reference to the tasks performed by the beluga. He believed that the unusual wear on their teeth and their dark color proved that the whale's masters had filed them. The Russians had explained this unusual trait as a severe inflammation of the gums that had required an operation and the removal of a piece of flesh on the lips. The truth may never be known, but Nessi believed the beluga had been trained as a saboteur and his teeth filed so that he could mouth large objects such as magnetic mines, which, at the risk of his life, he would affix unto the hulls of enemy ships and submarines.

At the Russian Embassy in Rome, no one apparently knew anything about the beluga, but an Italian employee put Nessi in touch with a friend of hers in Moscow, Volodya Vanin. Through him, Nessi was led to the institution responsible for the beluga, the Sverdrov Research Institute, and to its senior officer, Lev Mukhametov. For weeks, almost every day and without ever getting an answer, Nessi phoned, faxed, and wrote Mukhametov, asking for a meeting to arrange for the release of the whale. Nessi could not have known that what he was asking was quite in conflict with the institute's and Mukhametov's interests. Mukhametov was a dealer in whales. He provided specimens for various facilities at home and catered to aquaria in Argentina and Chile, to which he delivered dolphins from the Crimea, and to Japanese clients, who bought beluga whales from the Sea of Okhotsk.

Then one day, quite unexpectedly, Nessi was invited to Moscow. Mukhametov told him in good Italian that the whale had not been taken back to the military base but to a public oceanarium at Laspi in the Crimea, where he gave shows daily. And he announced that the whale was available . . . for $60,000 (U.S), the usual sum for a beluga in Japan. But all that Nessi could offer as payment was three hundred letters from among those he had received from the children of Europe. When he suggested he could find a smaller sum from Italian sponsors devoted to research and conservation of Black Sea marine mammals, Mukhametov asked him to come back in two months' time.

$\longleftarrow$

*O*n this next trip, Nessi was taken to see Palla di Neve in the Crimea. He was in a large enclosure, 160 by 80 feet, at the head of a small bay next to the harbor, along with two dolphins and the same young beluga he had escaped with from Sebastopol the previous fall. Presently, hundreds of jellyfish drifted in through the wire fence, swirling up and down whenever a whale swam by. The young beluga named Igor, still gray at three years of age, followed his older companion like a shadow. Mukhametov complained that in a newly independent Ukraine plagued by unemployment, energy shortages, and lack of many basic goods, crowds at the oceanarium were often so small that buying food for the animals was a problem. As he wondered why the Russians had recaptured the beluga in the first place, Nessi realized that he now had two belugas to free instead of one.

That summer and fall, Nessi labored through the logistics at home and flew again twice to Moscow and the Crimea with veterinarians to certify the good health of the animals and to conclude the deal with Mukhametov. The Russian had agreed to let the whales go but warned that they had to be moved from their enclosure before the stormy month of November. Meanwhile, in Italy the plan was stalled by a domestic war between environmental and political interests. And suddenly, on November 19, 1992, Nessi received a dramatic plea for help from Mukhametov: the pen in Laspi had been shattered by a storm that had again sent Palla di Neve into the open sea and had badly injured Igor.

Nessi flew to Moscow with a case of medical supplies, apprehensive about arriving after winter had already set in. Everything about his arrival served to increase his anxiety. Vnukovo Airport appeared to be in the midst of a vast migratory movement, overused and undercleaned, inhabited by crowds of people sprawling with bags, bundles, and assorted sleeping gear. Then Volodia announced that their flight to the Crimea had been canceled because of the chronic shortage of air fuel. He would not rent a car, since Nessi's visa did not include a thousand-mile itinerary by land through Russia and the Ukraine. But Nessi produced American dollars, which had an immediate effect on Volodia. Within half an hour, they were on the road to the Ukraine in a brand-new Toyota they had rented for two days, paying $600 (U.S.) cash in advance on the understanding that they would travel only within the Moscow area.

The car was nice, too nice. It attracted every single police patrol, which never seemed to stop any other cars but would release theirs for $2 (U.S.) per officer. The temperature hovered around five degrees Fahrenheit, there were no direction signs, and the highway was covered in snow and ice that melted into potholes as they progressed south. Long stretches of gray countryside were broken by rows of bulky and dilapidated tenement buildings interspersed with small, dark houses with tiny, fenced-in plots. Abandoned vehicles cluttered the roads, and the only food Volodia could procure were tiny brown loaves of bread that he obtained by waving one-dollar bills above lines that snaked around blocks. They entered Kharkov in the Ukraine late at night, and no hotel had a vacancy. Volodia asked Nessi to flash U.S. dollars, which procured them one tiny room with a single bed that a sleepy host had hastily vacated.

At five in the morning, they hit the long, flat road again, resuming their endless crossing of the former Soviet Union in full depression. As they had discovered the previous day, finding gas was the major worry. They had to look for cars parked on the roadside with their hoods and trunks ostentatiously open, showing metal tanks from which twenty liters of gas could be pumped in exchange for bottles of vodka or the equivalent in U.S. dollars. After encountering a last police squad to whom Nessi, having run out of dollar bills, paid two one-thousand lira notes, worth only fifty cents each, they finally came in sight of the Black Sea. It was still heavy with the aftermath of a storm whose ninety-mile-per-hour gusts had sunk ships and jerked the jetty at Yalta six inches off the shore. Miles of coastline had been destroyed, including the dolphin and beluga pen in the bay at Laspi.

Igor had been unable to follow the stronger Palla di Neve into the open sea. Like a small boat left at dock in a storm, he had been picked up by a huge wave and bashed against the concrete wall of the jetty. He was moved to a children's small swimming pool higher up on firm ground, where a veterinarian from Minsk had hastily sutured a large cut above his right eye, where the arch bone had been broken. The whale could not open his eye and was evidently in pain, but Nessi was unable to obtain more veterinary help locally or abroad. For three weeks, Nessi hopelessly tended the young whale while a military Mikojan helicopter made rounds over the sea to locate Palla di Neve. In the end, thoroughly depressed, Nessi decided to return home via Istanbul on the high-speed hydrofoil that sailed from Yalta overnight. He was the only Western European on board, most other passengers being portly women with huge bags and bundles full of hand-knit shawls, *matrioshka* dolls, and assorted crafts to be traded for brand-name clothes and other western rarities in the grand bazaar of Istanbul.

A few days before Christmas, Mukhametov wrote Nessi that Igor had fallen into a depressive mood, spending his days belly-up at the bottom of the dirty water of his small pool, surfacing only briefly to breathe. Nessi returned to the Ukraine, this time opting for the train from Moscow to the Crimea. It was a forty-hour trip interrupted by countless stops at stations tended by sleighs, where old women sold hot nuts, apples, and potatoes in iron pots to hungry passengers leaning out the car windows. This time, Nessi had brought his own food; offering a bribe to the train chief, he was allowed into the crew's galley, where he cooked and shared his kilogram of Barilla spaghetti and can of Cirio tomato sauce.

When Nessi arrived at Laspi, Igor was at the bottom of the pool but reacted to his presence and that of his trainer Alla by slowly emerging. He swam toward them, holding the injured side of his head out of the water, and made half a move toward a ball in the water, which led Nessi to hope that the whale was not irremediably lost. Not wanting to return home until he felt Igor was secure, Nessi spent Christmas in the Crimea, travelling between Laspi and his gloomy resort hotel in Yalta, where he ate uninviting food in a colossal dining room enlivened by stage shows and a constant flow of prostitutes.

All this time, Palla di Neve had been astray. He was reported in the fall by sailors on a ship of the Black Sea Command off Odessa in the Ukraine. No one claimed the 250,000-ruble reward offered by Mukhametov for information leading to his capture. Nessi, who kept in touch with the embassies of every country bordering the Black Sea, feared the beluga had been caught in a fishing net and drowned. In January, as no end to the discussions in

Italy were in sight, Mukhametov made the decision to return Igor to the military facility in Sebastopol.

⤺

Spring in Montréal came early. It was now almost exactly one year since I had been to Turkey, and I was once again without news of the white whale in the Black Sea. I had been gathering data on that body of water, and I now somewhat regretted having recommended leaving the beluga there. The Black Sea is a strange body of water, naturally devoid of oxygen and therefore of fish below a depth of 300 to 650 feet. This is due to the lack of mixing between deep water and the surface, and to the decomposition of the organic matter that sinks to the bottom. The situation is worsening due to the increasing input of organic particles from human activities in Turkey and along the main tributaries in the north, which still bear their romantic names: the Danube, the Dniester, the Dnieper, the Don. All are sources of industrial and agricultural chemicals, such as hydrocarbons, PCBs, and DDT, which end up in the fish as they do in the St. Lawrence. In May 1986, a cloud containing radioactive material reached the Black Sea from the meltdown of the nuclear reactor at Chernobyl. Since then, more radionuclides have arrived, mixed in with the waters of the Danube and the Dnieper, whose watersheds have been heavily impacted by this disaster.

Yet I believed returning the whale to Siberia was a gamble as well. None of my North American and European colleagues working on the beluga had been able to tell me what the situation of the species was in waters off northern Russia. The press was littered with stories on wild development, environmental disasters, and plunder of wildlife throughout Siberia. And so I sat at my desk in Montréal, another season on the St. Lawrence about to start, wondering where on earth one could find a safe place to return an animal to.

I felt as helpless as when I heard the news of another death on the St. Lawrence. I always wished there had been some bold move I could have made before it happened, to stop the slayer before it struck instead of dusting the mirror for prints after the damage had been done. I wished I were Emilio Nessi working the streets rather than a scientist in the lab. Above my desk hung a poster from the Shedd Aquarium in Chicago, showing two captive belugas in pastel colors. Like most other belugas in North American aquaria, they had been captured in Hudson Bay, Canada. But unlike others, these were about to take part in a research project aimed at understanding the health condition of St. Lawrence belugas.

Like all cetaceans in captivity, the Chicago whales had been trained to allow samples of their blood to be taken to monitor their health. The whales simply came near the edge of their pool, lifted their flukes, and allowed a needle to be inserted into a vein. I had just been on the phone with the Shedd Aquarium staff, scheduling the shipment of fresh samples to us. Sylvain De Guise would extract their white blood cells and store them in a deep freeze, where they would keep for months, becoming active again when thawed as required for experimenting. We were planning to expose these immune cells to the same toxic chemicals that circulated in the blood of the wild St. Lawrence whales, in the hope the cells' response would help us understand how disease began and progressed in our beleaguered whales.

This time, the samples were to be shipped to Holland's Pieterburen Seal Rehabilitation Center, where Sylvain was in residence to learn about some highly specialized techniques. I had just set up an account with the Dutch airline KLM to speed the delivery from O'Hare in Chicago to Schiphol Airport in Amsterdam. My latest messages to Sylvain about the arrangements had not been returned, and I was puzzled, hypnotized as I was by the Chicago poster on the wall. I felt uneasy about using captive animals for our own purposes. Not that I worried so much about their physical health. Husbandry techniques in North America have improved considerably since Mr. Barnum's time, and survival of captive belugas is, as far as we know, about the same as in the wild. The aquarium in New York, where so many belugas died in the 1960s, has recently bred the species with success.

I had ambivalent thoughts with respect to the captivity of cetaceans or of any wild animal, and I envied Emilio Nessi's determined and unconditional opposition to it. Even though my colleagues and I did not participate in captures or support them directly, our research needs helped legitimize the concept of keeping whales in artificial surroundings. I did believe in their use for educative and research purposes, and for whatever was learned that helped to protect wild herds, strengthen endangered species, or reestablish extinct populations through captive breeding. But there was a fine line between public education and public amusement, between what is good for us and what is good for the animals. I feared that one day I might not see that line and might cross it. I had read somewhere that captive animals were paying time so that others could keep on living in the wild. I hoped that the price was not too high.

My phone rang. It was Sylvain, and he stunned me: he was calling from Turkey! A few days before, the Pieterburen Center had received a phone call about a beluga whale, and its director asked for Sylvain because of his expertise with the species in Canada. Sylvain was told that a beluga had just been sighted off Turkey in the Black Sea, and someone by the name of Emilio

Nessi was requesting expert help. Sylvain answered that not only did he know of beluga whales, but he was also quite sure he knew this particular animal. Sylvain met Nessi at Istanbul Airport, and they immediately set off to Gerze and arrived on the pier after dawn. And there, exactly where Sylvain and Emilio had seen him the year before, was Palla di Neve, in good health, unmistakable with his lip scar, the prisoner who had escaped twice from Russian jails! His return had thrown the town of Gerze into a permanent fiesta. A special bank account was accepting donations toward sustaining the whale, and the harbormaster had set up a quality inspection procedure for the fish intended for the marine mammal. In the very center of town, a gigantic bronze torso of a famous Turkish general had been taken down to make room for a new wooden sculpture of a beluga whale.

Later that year, the Turkish Minister of Environment forbade the recapture of the animal within Turkish waters, and Palla di Neve, or Aydin, the beluga whale from Siberia, is still, to this day, roaming freely in the Black Sea.

⌐⟶

On board the nuclear submarine USS *Montana*, there was total silence, a standard procedure followed when in ambush or in the immediate presence of the enemy. Not allowed to talk, walk, or make any noise, the crew lay in their bunks, most men using the time to read. These prolonged bouts, which added discomfort to an already boring routine, had occurred frequently in the last several weeks, and officers and men were counting the hours until they would leave these waters and get back home. By now, they had been here for three months, lying still at the bottom of the Black Sea, listening to the traffic above their heads.

Fourteen weeks before, just after leaving its base in Norfolk, Virginia, the submarine had dived. As usual, it would remain submerged continuously for the next four months until it came back to its base. On its present mission, the submarine was headed due east beyond the other side of the Atlantic to the Strait of Gibraltar. The first part of the ride across the ocean and into the Mediterranean had been routine, following almost exactly the same latitude all the way to Sicily, a distance of over 4,500 miles. Going around the island and passing by the southern tip of Greece, the submarine had then meandered north through the countless islands of the Aegean Sea until it was off Kumkale on the Turkish coast, at the entrance of the strait of Dardanelles. From this point, slowly and quietly, it had started on its secret path northeast up the narrow channel into the Sea of Marmara and on toward Istanbul.

The first rays of the sun lit the tall minarets of the Blue Mosque on the hill in historic Istanbul when the USS *Montana* entered the Bosphorus. The immense city on either side was already busy, its streets clogging up with traffic, unaware of the craft silently passing Seraglio Point, hidden only a few feet above the bottom of the channel. Although the submarine was traveling a narrow and busy seaway, the executive officer was unconcerned. Unlike the captains of the many ships sailing on the surface, he had no other craft in his tridimensional slab of water, and the heavy traffic in the Bosphorus would overwhelm the noise of his own vessel. Beyond the rock wall on top of which stood Topkapi, the former palace of the sultan, the officer left the Golden Horn on his port side and veered to starboard to go between the pillars of the bridge linking Europe to Asia. There were only about twenty more miles to go in this narrow channel, which averaged one mile wide, before the submarine, flowing in with the current, arrived off the village of Rumeli Feneri. There, it would enter the Black Sea, where much caution would be required. Its target was the Soviet navy base around Kazachia Bay in Sebastopol. That is where the USS *Montana* would lie on the bottom for more than three months, listening to every sound and recording every movement of every ship of the Russo-Ukrainian armada.

⌒⃯

*M*eanwhile, the young beluga Igor was in the military facility at Sebastopol, and Nessi had not given up on his plan to get him out of there. First, he had to see for himself how the whale was doing, which required that he enter the home base of the Black Sea Command of the former Soviet Navy. In February 1994, he went to Yalta to devise a plan with sympathizers Volodia Vanin, Mukhametov, and a base resident. The base was a fortress, locked and closed not only to foreigners but even to nonresidents. Nessi was lent the passport of another base resident for three hundred dollars, and given a map showing a little-used exercise path that would take him out in three hours, should a problem occur within the base. Heart in throat, Nessi rode the sixty miles to the gate with his companions under strict orders never to utter a word. Compulsively, he kept his mind going over the map he had memorized, and tried not to think of what would happen if he were caught.

At the gate were three officers, representing the navy, the army, and the militia. Volodia handed in the four passports, placing Nessi's borrowed one under the pile. While the navy representative scrutinized the first passport, the heavy militia officer walked around the car with a great fierce-looking dog. Second passport, third passport. Nessi held his breath, on the verge of panic, when, out of nowhere, a group of cyclists in full competition garb caught everybody's attention. The guard handed back the passports, and with a salute, showed the visitors through the gate.

They drove through the base, which Nessi scanned intensely, trying to remember any detail that could be of use. Beyond the gate stretched wide-open areas planted with vineyards and single, peaceful, little white houses. Farther on were barracks where soldiers trained, with tanks and vehicles moving about, and sentinels on high towers scanning the ground below. Then there were radar towers along landing strips and bunkers in camouflage paint. Farther on, alongside a bay, scores of warships of all sizes were tied beam to beam. The clandestine visitors ended up on a small cove closed off from the sea on one side by a high concrete wall and on the other by a net tightly set along a line of rusted steel posts. Within that enclosure, an area was partitioned into ten or so individual empty pens, each a few square yards, as if to accomodate new guests expected in the coming days away from indiscrete eyes. Somewhere within that closed-in bay was Igor.

Suddenly, there he was at the surface, again a playful young beluga, perhaps a little whiter in color than before but in apparent good health, with only healed scars where his injuries had been. Mukhametov said that Igor's fate had not yet been determined. He would either be given military training with special ultrasonic equipment installed in the bay or be taken to a civilian facility in Moscow. Nessi, of course, was opposed to both plans.

〜

*T*he recent alert on board the USS *Montana* had been caused by an unexpected noise outside. Not the sound of a ship's engine but that of an underwater searching device, a sonar. It was feeble, though, unlike any onboard ships of the Soviet Navy. The sonar officer recognized it almost immediately as the voice of a whale. The animal was coming right toward the hull, sending trains of sounds at short intervals, obviously investigating. It came very close, straight ahead of the bulging bow of the submarine, and stopped, resting motionless, bouncing sound waves off the vessel.

The sonar officer took his headphones off, buzzed by the incessant ratchetlike voice of the whale. Like everyone else on board, he was anxious about having been detected and wondered what would happen next. At the same time, though, he smiled, because he was quite sure he knew what kind of whale was outside at the bow of the sub. It was a beluga whale, and it was scanning precisely at an engineered counterpart of itself. Like other nuclear submarines of the U.S. Navy, the bulge in the bow of the USS *Montana* had been developed from studies on beluga whales carried out at the Naval Ocean Systems centers in San Diego and Hawaii where researchers like Wayne Turl worked. This device gave American submarines a distinct advantage over their foe.

The domelike bulge was a highly sophisticated sonar array, a partial sphere with hundreds of transducers. Each of these electronic devices for sending and receiving sounds could be activated selectively by an operator inside the submarine to achieve a search pattern covering a very large volume of water in front of and to the sides of the submarine. This technological achievement had originated from the very simple observation that a beluga modifies the shape of its melon when echolocating. A dolphin moves its entire head in an approximate ellipse to scan a relatively small area, but a beluga orients its melon and, with a small vertical motion of its head, can more than double the space covered with narrow sound beams. This adaptation allows the whale to search a large volume of water in a very short time with minimal movements of its body. The same principle when applied to a submarine allowed it to find out where the enemy was without moving the ship sideways, thereby avoiding the risk of giving its presence away through the sound produced by the engine and propeller.

The beluga in midwater over the USS *Montana* was Palla di Neve. That day, passing in the vicinity, he had stopped to investigate the American vessel. Thus he had finally done one of the things he had been trained for: finding an alien submarine. But Palla di Neve no longer worked for the Russian navy. He worked for himself now, and he had more interesting things to do in the Black Sea. In a short while, he simply swam away, aimlessly headed toward the west and the shore near the mouth of the Danube River.

I returned to Turkey in the fall of 1994, not knowing what I was looking for, but longing for the sense of timelessness that came from its blend of ancient civilizations. I needed to go to the old quarter of Istanbul where weatherworn pieces of Greek, Roman, Turkish, and European cultures stand amid modern city growth like erratic boulders in a forest. One morning at dawn, I climbed up the narrow street that hugs the wall of the old sultan's palace toward the Roman basilica of St. Sophia, whose dark cupola lured me from the top of the hill. Built under Justinian in the sixth century, it was later flanked by minarets that are now old enough to make the whole seem coherent. Though I was walking through evidence of change, of civilizations replacing each other, a peaceful feeling of permanence pervaded, as if there were an equilibrium in man as there is one in nature, established after periods of clash that are no longer perceptible.

I arrived at the gardens behind the basilica to find the entrance nearly blocked by a string of chartered buses parked by the rusty

red walls of the colossal church. Asleep in their seats behind blan-
keted windows, dozens of Russian traders waited for the grand
bazaar to open. Like the vines on the walls, they belonged to the
modern living world. When the bronze gates of the grand bazaar
opened, they would flow downhill to wander through its maze of
Ottoman arches. They would gather perishable goods like food and
clothes or others that have symbolic values, from Rolling Stone
T-shirts to antique Coptic manuscripts, but all of them things that
could be bought and owned.

Beyond the site of the vanished hippodrome where the blues
and the greens fought to the death centuries ago, I went down the
winding streets of the Armenian quarter. It was drizzling softly over
young boys carrying on their heads gargantuan trays with neat piles
of baklavas and rose water pastries, over men slouching under bundles of bluish styrene jugs in pink plastic bags the size of hot-air
balloons. At noon I emerged onto Kumkapi, a fashionable fish market and seafood dining area by the boulevard on the Sea of Marmara. Only two narrow cobblestone streets lined with small,
spotless, and brightly lit restaurants. I ordered a uniquely Turkish
tomato salad and a grilled fish in a restaurant that had just been
renamed *Beyaz Balina*, the White Whale.

It was here that I understood what the true nature of the
beluga was: an endurable but fragile piece, much older than this
ancient city, one of a kind, and which could never be replaced.
Like St. Sophia, the beluga was part of man's precious heritage, to
be preserved at all cost. But unlike the antiques in the bazaar, it
could not be possessed and hoarded. It begged us to cherish what
we cannot get close to, cannot touch, hold, or control. The future
will judge our civilization not solely by its own works but also by
how we have lived in harmony with the natural world.

That day the beluga Aydin, or Palla di Neve, was somewhere
off Bulgaria, causing discontent among villagers over fishing

rights. He was free but had only limited rights. I had heard from Nessi that Igor was no longer in Sebastopol but in Moscow. He spent his days doing rounds and giving shows in the diving pool built for the 1980 Olympics, the games that the West boycotted over the now-forgotten war in Afghanistan. Like many things in Russia and everything in the bazaar here in Istanbul, Igor was for sale. I imagined that he must be hard to unload, like a famous painting stolen from a museum that cannot be sold openly.

It was raining on the stones in the square, and a waiter in his white shirt ran back from across the street with green lemons in his hand.

OPPOSITE PHOTO: Nyatamah, an adopted beluga, and her newborn calf, off Kamouraska Islands. Calves follow their mothers closely and are weaned after one or two years. (PHOTO CREDIT: DANIEL LEFEBVRE)

From the River to the Ark

〜〜〜

*C*ome July, the St. Lawrence has been tamed and is no longer forbidding. There is a stillness about the air that says summer is here at last and here to stay. The days are long, as they were in June, but the sun is warmer, its rays penetrating deeper into the river, whose water glows like the star in a sapphire. This is the time when older people dare go for a ride on the water to renew their friendship with the river of their youth. Younger people take to the water, too, for the river in July will give all it has. August will be lovely still, but it will have become too warm, the trees too heavy, the fields too thick with hay before the lingering summer ends in fog and gives way to the storms of September.

July is when we ponder whether our season of work on the whales will be a good one and if the river will hold its pledge to unravel something more of their lives. Since May, the hours have been long but the weeks short, for only one day out of three has been free of strong winds or fog. We have paid our dues, coming out whenever we could at daybreak and returning after sunset, knowing that whales are shown only to those who are out on the water.

Today was July 12, and we had hoped to record the sounds of whales. Since morning, we had patrolled up the north channel but all we had seen were two single belugas. After careful approaches, the engine was stopped and the underwater microphone lowered into the water, only to find that the whales were silent.

By noon, we were at the upstream spit of Hare Island, and, after veering around it inside the buoy, we coasted down the South Channel on the last hour of the ebb. There was hardly any wind, and the tide was just about to start rising. These were perfect conditions for recording, and we hoped belugas might be coming in on the tide from downstream. But the loudspeakers were still silent, and I would have been dispirited if it had not been for the warm air, which allowed me to take my overcoat and sweater off and to enjoy the sun. Now and then, there was a low rattle when the cord leading to the hydrophone vibrated in the water or rubbed against the hull. A hiss or screech sometimes came in from an unidentified source some distance away whose sound traveled on an acoustically favorable layer of water all the way to our boat. Otherwise, it was the beginning of a calm and quiet afternoon in the middle of the estuary of the St. Lawrence River, and there were no belugas around.

By two o'clock, the color of the river had changed under our hull and our determination had faded. I watched the brownish, murky waters from upstream being pushed back by cold green eddies that the tide had brought in from below. Flocks of gulls came in to sit on the water, waiting for fish to frisk where the salt-water surged. The ferry passed us on its way to the north shore, and soon our own small boat went drifting by Rivière-du-Loup, where the ship had come from. But nowhere were belugas to be seen or heard, and I was annoyed at the waste of a long day. We were about to give up and make a dash for Green Island farther down when the lookout on top of the cabin announced some belugas downstream. I swung my binoculars in that direction. There was a cluster of white spots two miles away, which could only mean a pod of beluga whales logging at the surface. The hydrophone was swiftly pulled in and we made for that site at low speed. Within a thousand feet of the whales, the engine was switched off and the hydrophone lowered into the water one more time.

We had come near a group of five or six white adults and two gray juveniles. None of the whales came to investigate the boat. The two young whales were actively swimming at some distance around the adults, who calmly bobbed at the surface very close together. Our drift brought us to within three hundred feet of them, a distance that allowed for a very thorough investigation with binoculars. Underwater, the hydrophone picked up only an occasional sound from the whales, and I asked for the loudspeaker volume to be turned up when I climbed atop the cabin. I was intrigued: I had never seen such a tight formation of adults seemingly at rest so close together in the middle of the day. As it turned out, we were about to witness an event that no one had ever observed and that we have not yet seen again.

At two twenty-five, we heard a sudden burst of sound as if all the belugas were squeaking, whistling, and gurgling at the same time. Beluga whales are the most vocal of marine mammals, and they can produce sounds both underwater and at the surface. Earlier in the season, at the break of day, we had encountered dozens of them at rest and dispersed over hundreds of square yards on the still water, like logs lost to the river by a passing ship during the night. Mixed in with their blows were an amazing variety of sounds that they produced with their vents. Here was a squeaking door and the wail of the wind through a window not tightly shut; there was the whistle of a mynah bird to which answered the rattle of a snake, the bark of a dog, and a cow passing wind. The composite sounds of animals fallen off Noah's ark.

Most whale sounds are produced underwater and do not break the water-atmosphere interface, which is as reflective of sound as a mirror is of light. Underwater sounds originate from vibrations in the air that is locked within the whale's nasal passages; the vibrations are then funneled out by the skull bones and the melon. Some sounds are of a very practical nature, such as clicks used for echolocating objects in their environment and for finding prey. Others are sounds used for communicating between individuals, sounds with a social purpose. These were the sounds we were interested in, for we thought they might help us to understand what belugas did when they were underwater—which is of course most of the time. Perhaps it may eventually be possible to associate given sounds with specific behaviors and to start deciphering the basics of beluga communication. There may even be specific calls distinguishing youth from adults, males from females, and—who knows?—individual whales. For weeks we had been recording belugas while noting the number of animals, their sizes and color, any identification marks and specific behavior. Gradually, we were building a list of their various sounds and calls, even though we did not understand what they meant. Presently, our list looked like a dictionary in an unknown language in which the words' definitions had not yet been entered.

What we were hearing today off Rivière-du-Loup was something different, as if the five or six whales in front of us were going at high speed through every phrase in their repertoire. The resulting sound was reminiscent of the blend of insect shrills and birdsongs in a rain forest. This underwater excitement, as transmitted by the hydrophone to the tape recorder on board, lasted for three minutes. Then, at two twenty-six, a tiny calf of brown to graybeige color rose on the back of an adult. It did not make any movements and appeared as listless as a rag doll. There were distinct folds on its side, the narrow flukes and pectorals were limp, and a pronounced hump stood on its head behind the blowhole, like those on stillborn calves I had seen on the beach. I barely had time to grasp what was happening when the calf, shining in the sunlight, slid off into the water like an inanimate object. I realized that we had just witnessed the first few minutes in the life of a beluga whale calf.

I could hardly believe it—a birth in the St. Lawrence, right before our eyes! But my joy was premature, for something seemed to have gone wrong. The calf did not move at all and appeared to be incapable of surfacing on its own. Repeatedly, it was brought back to the surface and held there on the head or on the back of an adult. Because the six adults were so close together, we could not determine if it was always the same whale that supported the calf. On one occasion, an adult touched the calf with its head as it was being held at the surface by another adult. Was the mother one of these two whales? That will never be known. At times, one of the two juveniles joined the group briefly and swiftly returned to its peripheral position with the other juvenile. It was as if the young gray animals were not allowed to participate in the momentous events that were happening at center stage. I was worried now. Seventeen minutes had gone by, and still the calf would not move but kept falling off its white slippery platform, like a piece of wet soap on the side of a tub.

Then, at two forty-three, the calf moved for the first time. Resting on the back of an adult, it lifted its flukes while twisting its body slightly. Both were quite unassured movements that sent the calf back into the water immediately. I was relieved. Now the calf was back at the surface once more, only half touching an adult and splashing the water with its tail. Perhaps the whales were relieved, too, for the loudspeakers were alive again with frequent sounds, some of quite high amplitude. At two forty-five, the loudspeakers transmitted the sound of jaw claps when a gray animal was seen approaching the group of adults and calf. This sound is generally interpreted as an aggressive behavior, and it seemed to confirm that the juveniles were not welcome anywhere near the calf.

A few minutes later, the group of adults drifted apart and moved away from the vicinity of the boat. The calf was no longer being held at the surface and could not be seen as often, but it was apparently holding on. When visible, it broke the surface on its own, very energetically, yet quite clumsily. It would come up obliquely as if about to surf or would exit vertically almost all the way up to its pectorals. Similar maneuvers have been observed among smaller calves of the year upon surfacing, as if they were not too sure exactly where their blowholes were, and made sure to raise their heads well out of the water before taking a good puff. Our little fellow seemed to be more capable now, and the hump at the back of his head was no longer as conspicuous, perhaps because the muscles controlling the melon kept it plump and filled the space on the forward section of the skull.

At two fifty, the group stopped, and the adults drew closer to each other again. We could not see their every move, for they were farther away than previously, but it was obvious that the calf appeared to be in trouble once more. Few sounds were being transmitted by the hydrophone, and the baby whale had gone limp again. For the next twenty minutes, just like earlier, the calf was repeatedly brought to the surface and held momentarily on the back of an adult, only to shortly fall back in. Perhaps the calf was only resting after his first big round of physical exercise, for the adult whales appeared calm and bobbed as peacefully as before, but that was not at all how we felt on the boat, where tension was almost palpable.

After twenty minutes, the group of whales swam off unhurriedly. A small wind had risen and visibility was reduced, but we did not wish to start the engine and get closer for fear of upsetting the whales. We could not ascertain whether the calf was doing well or if it was even still around. I peered intensely for its small, dark figure among the wavelets that the wind had started to build up. Now the whales had broken into three groups: one white adult with two juveniles; one juvenile alone (where did this fellow come from?); and five . . . no . . . six white adults (perhaps one more adult than previously) behind, swimming close together and . . . the calf! Phew! He had made it, and there he was, surfacing as if he was trying to fly right out of the water!

Half an hour later, the group of one adult and two juveniles parted and was not to be seen again. The remaining animals then ordered themselves as they would for the rest of the day: one white adult with the calf in front, five or six adults following together about one thousand feet behind, and finally the single gray juvenile cavorting around them. The calf remained close to the one adult, which we now presumed to be its mother, surfacing in unison with her or on his own in his previously clumsy fashion. Very few sounds were heard, although the whales behaved in a very coordinated way. For two and a half hours, they traveled in wide spirals, ending up some three to four miles upstream of the position where we first saw them. Whenever the presumed mother and calf changed direction, the small pod behind would follow without any cue ever recorded on our hydrophone. We did not see them stop anywhere along the way to allow the calf to nurse.

Earlier, the wide and deliberate movements of the belugas had often brought them close to our boat, at which time they would veer or dive, producing chains of bubbles, and reappear in another direction. Now, it was obvious that they purposefully avoided us, and our careful attempts at getting a closer look at the calf by moving far ahead of the whales and waiting silently for them to come near were all unsuccessful. Therefore, at five forty-five, having spent almost four hours with the pod and judging that we might be interfering, we left them and went to look for other whales.

It was weeks before all the excitement of that day and the actual observations that we had made were settled in my mind and I could properly interpret what we had seen. Although we had not actually witnessed the expulsion of the calf from its mother, there was no doubt that we had arrived on the scene minutes before the birth actually occurred. There were obvious clues, such as the fetal folds on the calf, and the hump on its head, as well as the sudden burst of sounds, which had been reported in captivity during the birth of a bottle-nosed dolphin. There were so few records of whale births in the wild that our own observation was extremely precious. In particular, the lifting of the calf to the surface and the presence of a number of adults engaged in supportive behavior toward the mother-and-calf pair were significant observations in the context of the St. Lawrence beluga population. I was reminded of related descriptions that I had read in the report of a beluga whale birth at the Vancouver Aquarium on July 13, 1977—almost the same day of the year as ours.

In that instance, there were only forty minutes of quite calm labor before the baby was born headfirst. The calf immediately made for the surface, where it found itself swimming among, bumping into, and sliding off one or the other of the three big whales (including the mother) in the pool, all in a boiling mass. Then it was not the mother but another young female who took the calf along for prolonged bouts of active swimming around the pool, and with whom the calf spent most of its time. It was again with this baby-sitter that a first futile attempt to nurse was made, a full five hours after birth. The calf actually nursed from its mother for the first time another three and a half hours later. And more than one day and one night went by before the mother delivered the last of the afterbirth and fully assumed her role, after which the surrogate mother was able to settle back into her usual routine.

Consequently, in our own observations, the one whale ahead that we had assumed to be the mother may not have been she at all. Quite possibly the group activity observed shortly before and after the birth might have been the usual behavior for the species. It might have been a necessary step leading to the self-identification of a suitable baby-sitter who would take over from the tired mother until she was ready to assume her role. The need for such behavior may be of much consequence in the St. Lawrence, where the beluga population is small and, in the area used by females and young in the summer, is mostly composed of small units of three individuals or fewer. Thus the few larger social groups that exist may be extremely important for ensuring the normal rearing and survival of calves in the first days after birth. It is imperative that we get to know these groups and their preferred habitats so that they can be protected. The birth had occurred only a few miles from the pier and marina at Rivière-du-Loup, an area where on a nice summer day dozens of small crafts come and go and there is much potential for disturbance. Originating from that marina and from a number of other harbors on the river, more and more boats every year take tourists out for whale-watching cruises. Considering that there are also hundreds of small vacation craft, there is a definite threat of disturbing the whales in the activity that is of the utmost significance for their survival.

I understand people's legitimate desire to see whales. Seeing the newborn calf with its tiny triangular flukes beating the air, and splashing the water to keep its hold on the slippery back of an adult, and later on taking its first few gulps of air, I sensed why humans are so fascinated with whales. There he was, just out of the womb, the same way we humans start our own lives, although unlike us the calf was still immersed in a liquid and weightless, not on land feeling the pull of gravity. Upon being born, each one of us had also made that same hungry, perhaps panicky rush for a first gulp of air, though we have no recollection of it. This the calf not only did that day but will do it countless times, having to remember to come to the surface for air every few minutes of the day and night for as long as he lives. Perhaps there lies the first power of our attraction to the whale: it is the sound of the animal releasing and taking air that draws us into its world and back to the womb.

Then comes the knowledge that it is impossible for our species to follow the whale under the sea and survive. It is a world forbidden to us unless special equipment is worn, unless we are locked inside a cold metal sphere that can take the pressure, unless we turn into clumsy astronauts. We become fully aware that in some way the whale is a far superior being, for it can live at the surface or in the deep and it will not be crushed, its powerful heart will pump rich blood, and its lungs will not want for air for another hour. And when oxygen is needed, the whale can muster a powerhouse of muscles to reach for the surface in minutes from a thousand feet below and not get sick or die from decompression.

That is truly when, upon finally seeing it at the surface, the whale catches us and holds us. It is big, and we know it must be a powerful animal, for its blow is like cannon. And we fear somehow that it may overturn our boat unknowingly, like a friendly giant, or even worse, on purpose, for what is unfamiliar may be evil. Deep inside us there lurks the fear of the monster, the dragon, the dinosaur. And the whale is reptilian in a way, since unlike most other mammals, it has no fur; its skin is slippery and cold to the touch. And then the whale has gone under again, and we know that we cannot grasp it in any sense of the word. It will remain mostly invisible, hidden, showing us only a little piece of itself at a time, and we would have to spend a lifetime on the quick-tempered sea to get to know it well.

I do not know whether the calf that I saw being born is still alive this day and has grown into a gray juvenile and then into a white adult. As in many other long-lived mammals, the first few months in the life of a beluga are when it is most likely to die. Among the beluga carcasses retrieved from the St. Lawrence shore, many have been calves in their first year of life, most having died only days or weeks after birth. Beluga calves anywhere face many natural threats such as predators, disease, and perhaps a dependence on adults that leave them defenseless when separated from their herd by storms, by the moving ice floes, or through human interference. In the St. Lawrence, there is a most appalling additional threat, that of being intoxicated by their mothers' milk.

Beluga milk is very rich and may contain up to 50 percent fat. Unfortunately, fat is a good solvent for a variety of organic chemicals synthesized by man for industrial and agricultural purposes.

Such are the infamous polychlorobiphenyls or PCBs, DDT, dieldrin, mirex, chlordane, hexachlorobenzene, and more, which have been sprayed on fields or dumped underground or in streams. Some of these chemicals are almost indestructible by natural processes and remain in the aquatic environment until taken up by animals along with their food. Because most animals excrete very little of these chemicals, the compounds accumulate within the fat in their tissues. A mother beluga has a huge reservoir of fat in her blubber, which represents more than one-third of her total body weight of 1,300–2,000 pounds. In that blubber are stored almost all the toxic organics present in the food she has eaten since her birth. When her body produces milk for a calf, some of the toxics in the blubber are reclaimed along with the fat going into the milk.

In the dead females that we have examined, the amount of toxics in the milk was two to three times smaller than in the blubber. But that is still sufficient to intoxicate the calf, for he is a much smaller animal and milk is his only source of food. The milk contained on average ten parts per million of PCBs and six parts per million of DDT. This may look like only some cryptic number, but fish containing five times fewer PCBs is considered unfit for human consumption. A beluga calf will feed exclusively on such milk for up to one year, and it will need a lot of it to follow his mother along and to grow. At birth, the calf weighs only one hundred pounds or so, and he will reach almost 450 pounds by the end of his first year. That will, however, amount to only one quarter to one-fifth his mother's weight, and he will consequently end up being more contaminated than her. The nutrients and fat in the milk are metabolized by the calf, but the toxics are not; these will be stored in his blubber. In fact, toxic St. Lawrence fish would be a healthier diet than his mother's milk. In ecological terms, calves are feeding at a level in the food pyramid above that of their mothers.

Many calves do not make it to weaning. I know this because I have seen a number of them on the beach. The most contaminated belugas in my Book of the Dead were less than two years old, and several were little corpses of newborns that had not breathed for more than a few days. This is something that a pathologist can tell even if he has never been at sea to watch whales. When the fetus is still in the womb, its lungs are collapsed and contain no air. They will expand with the first breathing reflex, which is triggered by a sudden lack of oxygen in the blood after the fetus is expelled from the womb and facilitated by a natural surfactant that helps the inside linings of the lung alveolis part from each other and allow air in. Whatever is present in the tissues of a stillborn calf is the result of what had been happening inside the womb as opposed to within the river. Thus, if they bear toxic chemicals, it can confidently be said that these were transferred to the calf directly through the blood and the placenta of the mother. That is what we have found in a number of animals who, even though they had never taken milk and never eaten anything from the St. Lawrence, already had PCBs, DDT, and other chemicals in whatever little blubber there was under their wrinkled skins. That is the legacy that female beluga whales in the St. Lawrence are transmitting to their offspring, along with their genes. First in the womb and then through milk, toxic chemicals are passed on to the next generation like a family heirloom.

I had a long and precious encounter with one of these unfortunate and doomed calves. On the morning of August 6, 1992, a young man was walking on the beach around a small bay in Park du Bic on the south shore when he heard gulls squeaking a few feet above the breakers ahead of him. When he got closer, he noticed a form like a small log a few feet long being rolled in the muddied water. A herring gull was about to land on it, feet

extended, head bent down, ready to pick at it with its bill. Finding this interest in a log rather unusual for a gull, the man walked
closer and thought he saw the form move and twist on its own.
Then he recognized a head, the head of a seal, or rather that of a
small dolphin or porpoise. He rushed toward it, scaring the gulls
away momentarily, and realized that it was gray, not black, and
that it had no dorsal fin. It was a beluga calf, and it was alive.

When the man touched the calf, it produced shrill cries and
wriggled away. It seemed vigorous, yet could not or would not beat
its way through the breakers and back to the bay and out into the
St. Lawrence, where it had come from. There were cuts on its body
where it had been rolled against rocks and a bleeding wound near
the eye, which the man assumed had been caused by the gulls. He
looked out over the water, searching for an adult, for the mother,
for a sign of the presence of another whale in the vicinity. There
was nothing on the bay, nothing among the boulders on the other
side but driftwood and dead seaweed on the beach all the way
around to where he stood with cold, wet feet, next to a tiny shriek-
ing calf for which he now felt responsible. The man ran back several hundred feet to his car and then rushed to the warden's office.
Both returned immediately to the site, where the calf was still grap-
pling with the waves and the gulls. Now they felt as helpless as
anyone would have and uncertain whether to let nature have its
way or to try to assist the calf. But if they were to do anything,
they had to make their decision fast.

I was at home in Montréal that morning when Richard Plante
phoned about the calf. Richard was excited by the news of a live
whale on the beach. Without a moment's hesitation, I immediately sent him and a veterinarian to the site to assess the situation.
I then got in touch with the Montréal Biodome, a living museum
housing many animals in natural settings. They had the nearest
medical pool suitable for a cetacean, and we had already made

arrangements there for such an emergency. Then I sat down to think about what it was exactly that we had just set in motion.

According to the description, it was definitely a calf of the year and most likely a newborn—in either case, an animal unable to fend for itself. No adult whale had been seen in the vicinity, a strong suggestion that the calf may have become lost or abandoned outside of the bay in the St. Lawrence proper, which is twenty miles wide and very cold in that region. This meant that the calf had been on his own in open water quite some time, in addition to the hours spent in the surf. Presently, the tide was going down, the wind was still steady, and the calf would soon die of hypothermia and lack of food. Without the intervention of the young man, it would perhaps already have been disposed of by the gulls, who, perched on a rock that the tide was uncovering, did not seem to have lost any interest in their prey.

Unfortunately, taking the calf into captivity was not much more promising. Previous attempts at saving newborn cetaceans elsewhere had failed. We ourselves, the previous year, had tried to save a newborn male beluga found abandoned in similar circumstances on the other side of the St. Lawrence. We had nursed him and stood by him around the clock for ten days, only to see him die quite suddenly after we believed that the most difficult period had passed. Even assuming that the whale survived this time, it would not be weaned until six months to one year later, and would then have to be trained to catch its own prey in the wild. Eventually, it would have to be certified free of disease and fit to be returned to the river. Failing that, we would in the end simply have produced one more captive whale and achieved nothing of significance for the wild population it had come from.

As I waited anxiously by the phone, I was reminded of some negative press the previous year. There had been those who said that the whale should have been left on the shore where nature would have taken care of it in its own way. I could not share this dilettante attitude. For the last decade, my colleagues and I had been exposed to the health problems of the belugas, becoming aware of their plight—even, one might say, caring for their dead. In a way, every one of those deaths had been nature's own doing, but we had uncovered evidence that man had given nature not a little help with his impact on the river. For someone who was striving to save the wild population of beluga whales as a whole, it did not make much sense to be told to turn my eyes away from one of its individuals in need. Clearly, on both ethical and scientific grounds, there was nothing else to do but to try to get this calf off the beach as quickly as possible.

After obtaining all necessary governmental authorizations—a slow process—the whale was prepared for a three hundred-mile trip up the St. Lawrence, from a wild bay to an urban sprawl of three million people. We decided to move the calf by land, since flying it, including transfers by road, would have required at least three hours, not counting the uncertain delays in finding a charter plane. Traveling on land, the whale would be handled only once and would arrive almost certainly within five hours. So it was that the calf was laid in a truck, the same one that had been carrying its dead kin so far, except that this one was not in the trailer or in the box behind, but on the seat and alive. I could only hope that it would make it, for I had no desire to attend to its autopsy when it arrived later that night. Veterinarian pathologist Sylvain De Guise left Montréal at once to meet the whale halfway up the road. And I waited, waited.

My phone rang around midnight, announcing that the whale would be arriving at the Biodome any minute. I jumped into the car along with my wife Marie. On the first corner, the traffic light was red, but there was no one around, so I made a left turn through it. At the next corner, another red light, still no one around, and another illegal left turn. Instinctively, I checked my rearview mirror: *damn!* A police car was coming right behind me with its flashing blue-and-red lights. I pulled over immediately, put my hand brake on, and got out as the police car was barely stopping behind me. I ran to the officer behind the wheel and said in a single breath as he was winding his window down: *This is an emergency! I am rushing to the Biodome for a baby beluga that has just been on the road for five hours, and it must be in a terrible shape! Follow me!* And, without waiting for an answer, I ran back to my car, driving off immediately. In my rearview mirror, I saw the police car make a U-turn and drive away, and I heard Marie say: *I'll have to remember that excuse!*

We parked behind the Biodome only minutes before the calf arrived. I could see its shape through the window, lying on the back seat with a foam mattress partly wrapped around its body and kept wet throughout the trip. A clear plastic tube came out of its mouth, through which water with salts and glucose had been administered to the tiny animal at intervals since it had been retrieved from the beach. Richard's only words were, *It's a female, and she is small!* When I helped him and Sylvain get her out of the truck, I was appalled. There were well-defined creases on one side, fetal folds showing where the main body of the calf had been bent over while in the womb. That was definite evidence that she had been born very recently. But more than that, she was so tiny and so apparently thin: less than five feet long and weighing about eighty pounds! A premature birth . . .

We carried her carefully inside to the medical pool where Biodome veterinarian Jacques Dancosse and an attendant were already in the water. A careful examination showed several superficial wounds scattered over her body, and three particularly worrying, heavily chaffed areas on her belly, under the mandible, and near the eye. These were dressed with antifungal ointment and she was given an injection of antibiotics. She was then fed her first meal of a special milk formula enriched with vegetable oil and glucose. This was a tedious and delicate procedure that required inserting a tube down her throat and into her stomach to pour down the formula, following the usual practice with unweaned cetaceans. All that time, the calf screamed several times and tried to fight away, two good signs that she was still quite alive. When released, she swam off vigorously across the pool, hitting the wall, and then veered to swim around her new domain.

From then on, the baby female swam constantly, circling around the thirty-six-foot–diameter pool. She kept bumping against the side of the pool and her head became irritated, so a foam helmet was custom-made to protect her rostrum. She wore it almost all the time, giving her the look of a war casualty. The calf was left free to move around but had to be cornered and restrained at regular intervals for routine examinations, blood sampling, wound dressing, and the delicate process of forcefeeding her. A team of volunteers had been mustered to work in pairs for four-to-six-hour shifts around the clock, at least one person being in the water all the time to give the calf the comfort of a live presence. Some team members had not been exposed to belugas before, while others had so far catered only to dead whales—Sylvain De Guise, Daniel Martineau, and myself.

I found my hours of watch magical and very uplifting. I felt like a child when donning a wetsuit, disinfecting, and entering the pool. I would let myself float around in the half-lit room in the middle of the night, with the tiny beluga cruising around me. I would drift toward her path until she brushed against me, and at times I would watch her swim right up to me and push very vigorously against my hands when I held her head. Touching her pearl-gray skin was very much like running my fingers over wet glossy plastic; it felt as cool as the water. That was reassuring, indicating that she was not losing heat. I was fascinated with her short breaths, each one a hurried affair, as whales' blows always are, even when they are resting at the surface. It is all done in a flash—the vent opening like a valve to expel the spent air and take a fresh breath in, then swiftly shutting so tightly, like the blink of an eye. With a diving mask, I could follow her movement underwater as she glided effortlessly under the push of her tiny but powerful flukes, her bruised little piglet and inscrutable eye never moving in its socket, leaving me unable to tell if she felt scared or lost or whether she was happy to have been born to alien parents in rubber suits.

There was much optimism on the fifth day when the calf was still very active and strong, her wounds healing and her blood parameters good. But around midnight, while I was off duty, I received a dreadful call at home. The calf had just died, and like all other belugas that I had handled before, she was now waiting for me on a necropsy table. I drove to the Biodome with Marie, this time forgetting to move forward on green lights. The autopsy that night was a sad affair. Perhaps it was the presence of new people who were not hardened to this moment of truth when one is face-to-face with a real animal who has stopped breathing and there is nothing one can do. Or perhaps it was that this time there were too many of us who felt we had just lost a wild animal that we knew personally. As we opened this tiny whale that looked lost on the table, I missed Richard and I missed the river, and I, too, felt lost and so did Sylvain and Jacques, both of whom had put so much hope in this calf, and Marie, who had taken it all up onto herself as usual.

The death had been caused by a malformation of the larynx that made possible the entry of milk into the lungs, simply choking the animal to death. This was no spectacular death and not one that could be related directly to pollutants this time, although this calf was quite like the other belugas that had come to rest on this table. She carried her own toxic burden, as we discovered when samples of her blubber came back from the laboratory a few weeks later. They contained the highest levels of PCBs and pesticides that we had ever found in a newborn. This meant that the mother was very highly contaminated herself and, had she lived, would have fed her offspring highly toxic milk. The calf was doomed, therefore, but I felt much respect for a premature animal that had survived quite some time alone in the cold St. Lawrence, then traveled in a truck for five hours, and swum strong for five days, a clear demonstration that wild animals can make it if given a chance.

About a month and a half later, the carcass of a twenty-one-year-old female landed on a beach downstream of where the calf had been rescued. She had pneumonia, her stomach and intestine were ulcerated, and there were abcesses and nodules in her thyroid and adrenal glands. The female was lactating, although her mammary glands were heavily infected. She may not have been the mother of our calf, but she obviously had given birth to one, too, which would have found itself abandoned as well.

There are a few such mothers in my Book of the Dead who were in poor health and had died while giving birth, the calf being expelled from the womb and ending up alone in the great St. Lawrence next to a corpse. I have had ample time to think about these dying whales during all those years when I drove along the river pulling dead ones behind me. I wondered whether sick animals only gave up when the pain became unbearable and they were too exhausted to keep on. Some were females living within social groups, and as they fell back, then perhaps another whale would take charge of the calf for a few days until it died of inanition.

Others were lone animals, and maybe the last blow was a storm that put too much demand on them and separated the calf from its mother. I imagined them swimming through their ordeal in the silent way of animals. I still have no answers to these questions, for they are not things that trained biologists investigate. Like everyone else, I am only competent to ask such questions about my own species: how disease can be painful and debilitating, and how one's parents get old and disabled and then die. These are not legitimate queries when dealing with wild animals, not as individuals but only as statistics. Another one of these innumerable everyday things of life.

I left the Biodome at dawn with Marie and we roamed along quiet streets toward Mount Royal, an ancient volcanic hill in the middle of the city. From its summit, we watched the lights of the downtown high-rises fading away as daylight grew. The St. Lawrence rose behind them among the piers and the cranes and the bridges linking the human dwellings on either side. A long cargo ship was passing under the last bridge and exiting the locks of the seaway on its way up to the Great Lakes. That is where most of the water that flows past Montréal was coming from, and until it became much cleaner, there would be no healthy future for belugas.

The sun rose through a haze over the vast plain of the St. Lawrence valley. There were whales here ten thousand years ago—humpbacks, fin whales, bowheads, narwhals, belugas—and their blows echoed against the hill where I now stood surrounded by tall buildings. Their time has gone. The climate changed, the sea became river, and only belugas kept coming from time to time as far as the rapids where the bridge is now. The river is no longer theirs. It belongs to those who are now waking up in the city, coming out of their dens onto the streets, jogging on the mountain paths among the oak and maple trees. In a few hours, coffee and croissants will be served in the cafés and the shops will open, and it is going to be a beautiful day in the market with the flowers and the firm and full fruits and vegetables of August.

An old lady ambled by, walking her dog, and the animal came to greet us. It was clean and well-behaved, obedient to its master, an animal living in its own time and with a future. There are many like him in this city, animals that man has adopted, and they are faring well. It is only a matter of selection, for many animals are not easy to handle and others quickly become pests. If one does it properly, one can hold quite a diversity of them, as the Biodome does. When it opens in a few hours, parents will take their children to behold hundreds of plants and animals living together above stacks of life-support systems. Now here is a place with a future, where animals can be organized into simple ecosystems through which people can walk safely. There ought to be more of those here and there to accomodate well-planned families of animals. I wonder how many could be fitted into one of the high-rises in downtown—one floor with offices, one with animals, one with living quarters for humans.

In the Biodome, there is a rain forest with marmosets and capybaras. The real rain forest is vanishing, so this little one here in the middle of town will make people think about it. Next to the rain forest in the Biodome is a Laurentian forest with a beaver lodge. Now that is an achievement! Normally you would have to travel thousands of miles to see both kinds of ecosystems. The Laurentian forest is our own local forest, and if I walked to the other side of my hill this morning, I would look out north toward the Laurentian mountains, which, by definition, are covered with forest for thousands of square miles. It cannot be vanishing, can it? Well, you never know. Might as well prepare our children and teach them how to grow our forest indoors.

A sailboat glides down from the old harbor. It might be going all the way to Tadoussac, which will be a very nice trip until the end of August. Its crew may see whales, though they are bound to run into some fog and not see much of the seabirds and shore life. I wish I could tell them to turn left beyond the next bridge and to sail right into the Biodome. It also houses a St. Lawrence ecosystem, with gannets and fish and sea anemones and urchins and a little tongue of a beach with real waves and birds nesting on a tiny spit of groomed sand and beach grass. You never know, one day we may have to reproduce a mighty river in a tank. Presently, the small St. Lawrence ecosystem in the Biodome looks just like the real one may tomorrow. There are no belugas in it.

OPPOSITE PHOTO: Adult beluga whale cruising by to investigate the research boat. October 1995. (PHOTO CREDIT: DANIEL LEFEBVRE)

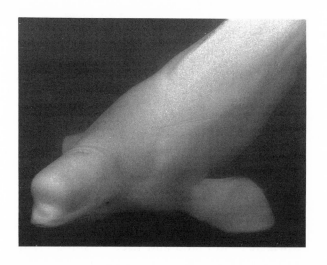

A Farewell to Whales

For many years, I spent much of my time thinking about belugas. Day and night, worrying. When I lay in bed, I would wonder where they were and what they were doing at that particular time. I have often left my car by the road and walked through the snow in hope of seeing a beluga from a hill overlooking the river, only to find it covered in ice for as far as I could see. I have taken the ferry many times in the off-season to check on the whales' whereabouts when our own research boat was in dry dock. I have wandered around marinas, mustering strangers to help me find a corpse among the waves, which sometimes we could not find. I have stood on the pier at Rivière-Ouelle in fierce winds to show friends where the whales were slaughtered for their oil.

This travail occupied long hours during which my mind would ease the pain by dwelling on the rosier sides of the life of the whale. Some thoughts were amenable to scientific scrutiny, such as whether belugas could detect thin ice through which to break for air by the volume of sound reflected from entrapped air bubbles. Others were questions that humans cannot hope to ever comprehend, such as whether whales are uncomfortable in choppy seas or, on the contrary, like to be rocked. And when I fell asleep, I would sometimes dream of a herd of white whales pursued by boats with gunmen until they were driven to the shore. The whales wiggled onto land and tried to slip away like giant snakes among the trees of the forest, but the men turned into wolves who ran after them.

But I can no longer bear to brood over belugas, and the time has come to exorcise my bad dreams. I have come to say farewell, for I have reached the conclusion that they are doomed in the world we humans are building. Not only belugas of the St. Lawrence, but all whales. And not only whales are in danger, since our lives have become estranged from wild animals and from wilderness.

On an average day, some two to four thousand calves are born to the various species of whales and dolphins that live throughout the seven seas. Some will grow to be as big as blue whales weighing one hundred tons; others will remain but tiny harbor porpoises less than one hundred pounds. They will be black, brown, blue, white, or gray to match the color or mood of the large rivers, the inland seas, or the oceans in which they live, and there will even be pink ones in the Amazon. From the warm tropics to the icy poles, they will search the mud and rub against pebbles, or they will roam through miles of water without any knowledge of shores or solid ground. Altogether, these calves represent about seventy-five different species, yet they have similar needs, and each will have come to the surface countless times for air before it dies. Soon, however, I fear they will be groping for water as well.

Clean water, that is, and water that can provide them with enough healthy fish. Within their different domains, all whales are dependent on the marine food chains—they lack other alternatives. In their everyday lives, they are competing with each other as well as with other animal forms, whether they be fish, birds, or seals, which, like whales, have no other possible way of life. At the same time, like all these other marine species, whales are competing with one other species, man, who has many alternatives but who exploits every one of them to its limit. That is partly a question of greed and of cultural attitude, but it is in the end dictated by our ever-increasing population. On an average day, that single competitor of whales will have taken 175,000 tons of fish from the oceans, moved 80 million tons of dirt and rocks on the globe, dumped 2 million tons of organic domestic garbage, and uncounted industrial refuse and chemicals that often end up in the sea. The huge refuse site on Staten Island has recently surpassed the Great Wall of China as the most voluminous man-made creation on earth. Every day, humanity gives birth to eighty thousand new individuals of our own species. That is twenty to forty times as many human births as there are births of all species of whales and dolphins combined. It can only be a matter of time before the latter are completely overwhelmed.

Many of the new humans arriving on the planet every day do not have much of a future, either. They are those who fell rain forest for subsistence agriculture, cut bush for charcoal to be sold by the roadside, or use mercury to sort particles of gold at the bottom of tropical rivers. Dying in their wake are the plants and animals that lived in the trees and on the soil that is washed to the river, where more wildlife will die from eating the fish contaminated with mercury. Yet these people cannot be blamed, for their wretchedness is not their own doing, and once they have been put on the list of the living, they have the same basic rights as any other human being. Their are simply trying to meet their basic needs, but the consequence is that the fate of much wildlife will in the end be determined by the world's poorest people.

The future of wildlife also rests in the hands of the not-so-poor who buy the gold, the charcoal, and the wood. The world has become one big market where the priviledged are buying raw materials for which they pay in dreams. The most valued dream is that development will provide everyone with a house, a car, a television set, and the support systems to manufacture, build, transport, stock, and sell the assorted goods and spare parts that come with them. And someday, on holiday, we will all ski the Alps and climb Mount Everest, go down into caves, jetboat up the Amazon and back down the Ganges, with hotels and tour buses to take us to the ends of the world, where we will trek in vain to the last unspoiled vista. It is to fulfill this dream that billions of goods and trinkets travel to world markets in cargo trucks, cargo trains, cargo jets, and cargo ships. And when one of them founders, an armada of running shoes or rubber ducks floats across an ocean on its own to end up on the beaches, if not in the stomach of a whale.

And there is the trade in wildlife, whereby the rich buy, the not-so-rich sell, and the poor do the poaching. In the end, as in the beginning, all men are equal. A few years ago, there was a beluga whale in the Black Sea that well-meaning people wanted to see rehabilitated and returned to its natural environment. That happened to be the Sea of Okhotsk off Siberia, Russia, and the beluga would therefore have found itself in one of the many countries where international animal genocide is occurring, epitomized by the Moscow bird market, which offers much more than feathered animals. In its precincts, an enormous variety of exotic animals from all over the world, several of which are endangered, if not already dead, change hands, whole or in parts. The dynamics of trade ensure that the rarer an animal becomes, the higher its value and, therefore, the greater the incentive to go and collect it in its habitat. It has been said that there are even chimpanzees and lemurs on the Moscow market, but if you cannot find what you are looking for, you can place an order, whether it be for ginseng, walrus ivory, tiger furs, sea otters. Or beluga whales.

I have tried for years to find peace of mind and to stop worrying. Of course, the whales may well survive longer than I will as an individual. I knew that all along, but I was naively thinking further ahead, focusing on beluga whales as only one example of threatened wildlife. Perhaps I might agree to giving whales up right away if doing so could save the rest. After all, whales may simply be the dinosaurs of today. And, elephants too. But then, what stories would I tell my grandchildren? Now, if I tell my child a dinosaur story, she may ask if they are real, and I can reassure her by saying that, although they were alive in the past, they do not exist anymore. I do not wish to be there when, being told an elephant story, children will ask if they are real.

Lately, I have found relief in telling myself a story. I already know how it goes, for I have told it many times. There is nothing like the comfort of one's favorite story, about which one knows every development and, especially, the way it ends.

THE TALE OF AKHBAR HONA

Sometime in another age, on planet Earth, there were, like today, humans everywhere, only they were more numerous. They had fortunately become wise and had solved the age-old plagues of war and famine, and there was no uncontrolled use and destruction of land. Trees were felled but forests were not cleared, fields were cropped but not eroded, dry lands were watered and tilled, and lakes were cleaned and groomed. People worked all year save for an annual leave to which everyone was entitled.

This new order had been achieved at high cost. Much of the surface of the planet was taken up by cities, suburbs, industries, roads, and airports, fields for crops, ponds and lagoons for growing seaweed and fish. There were many such landmarks on mountains and within deserts and under oceans. The remaining areas were for the most part vacationlands with hotels, golf courses, pools, water slides, campsites, ski resorts, miniature golf courses, shooting ranges, and the like. What little remained of grasslands, deserts, and mountains were thoroughly labeled, protected, and properly managed in a well-ordered way. There were thus no truly wild areas where one could go to find one's identity by slipping away from the presence of man.

In the process of establishing this new order, many plant and animal species had disappeared when their habitats had been gradually transformed to make room for the needs of a growing human population. Some of the extinct species had been cherished by many, and their disappearance had caused much grief among people. Therefore, those that remained had been afforded total protection and were closely monitored by the international community as an integral part of man's heritage. Any threat of extinction of any species because of new human settlements or provision of new services had to be submitted to and approved by the highest assembly of the people. And this was usually a very lengthy process. Our tale starts precisely at a moment when such requests had been made and a special meeting of the General Assembly of the United Nations in New York had been convened.

A number of countries from each continent had made requests for the reallocation of an area within their own territories that was still used by wild animals. Each request inferred the risk of losing a given species particular to that area. After long discussions among heads of states, it had been agreed that only a single permit would be granted and that it would be chosen by a vote in the General Assembly. On the appointed date, ambassadors from every country had arrived in New York, including those from the new countries in Antarctica. Each one wore his national headdress, which was designed to represent a typical wild species from his own country. These were to be worn throughout the proceedings, for there were no country names on desks and one had to know his hats in order to tell who was who among the hundreds of caps, bowlers, turbans, tiaras, and cloches of every color and fabric.

When all had been seated, the president went to the podium to announce that in accordance with the international constitution, it had been decided that only one area would be permitted to become civilized, and that only one last species would be allowed to risk becoming extinct. For forty days and forty nights ambassadors came in turn to the podium, many of them several times. Each pleaded either for the use of a given space within his own country, the selection of one in another country, or the necessity of sparing a particular animal, which consequently eliminated many of the areas under consideration. Whenever the name of an animal came up as a possible target, someone could be found who would defend that species on one ground or another. So it was that after all that time, no agreement had been reached.

On the morning of the forty-first day, Ambassador Akhbar Hona requested the floor. There was a hush in the grand room, for during the whole proceedings, Hona had remained in his seat, listening to every speech, without ever uttering a word. He was the ambassador from a small, dry country whose people dutifully nurtured their patch of desert in order to sustain themselves. He was a very wise and respected man whom everyone listened to. "It seems," said he in a soft and low voice, "that we are unable to reach a consensus. May I propose a way out of this dilemma? Since it is the disappearance of an animal that is at stake, perhaps it would be preferable to let the animals decide themselves. Therefore, I suggest that we should gather the representatives of all species of animals on the planet and ask them to make their own decision." Murmurs of approval came from across the room, and the president requested a vote on Hona's proposal. It was carried out immediately, in the customary manner of lifting one's hat above one's head as a sign of approval. Not one head remained covered, including that of the ambassador from McMurdo, who lifted very high the long cone of his emperor penguin headdress.

A huge ship was built in the harbor next to the Statue of Liberty, which in a short time became dwarfed by the growing craft. On its numerous decks, basins, stalls, gardens of trees and flowers, fields of grasses, hollowed rocks, tubes and jars of mud, and mats of decaying leaves were fitted up, provided by suppliers from around the world to house the representatives of every animal species. When the ship was ready and her crew chosen, she sailed under the captainship of able and wise Akhbar Hona. On a bright September morning, she left her berth by Liberty under the eyes of the ambassadors in their multicolored hats, and she was waved at by the crowds that had gathered on every pier all the way to the Atlantic.

The ship was at sea for months, visiting every port to gather one of every animal still alive on earth. Each was given his own kind of cabin as required by his taste and way of life. Then, having landed on six continents and traveled the seven seas, the ship came back to New York and to the crowds that had gathered in hope of a peep at some rare animal and to hear the bands and to see the kings and emperors and heads of states with their ambassadors around the Statue of Liberty. As soon as the gangway had been lowered, the president of the United Nations came on board to meet with Akhbar Hona and his animals.

He welcomed the animals, an assortment of beings the likes of which he had never seen before, and many among whom seemed quite preoccupied with eating their own special food while the president talked. He explained to them that it had been agreed they should be the ones to select the single species on the ship that would be required to give its place away. He told them to meet and to discuss the matter among themselves as long as would be necessary, not to count time, and to spare no expense. When they were ready to vote, he asked them to cast their secret ballot in the special box on the bow. It would remain sealed and under the care of Ambassador Hona until each animal had voted. Then the box would be taken to the United Nations, where the ballots would be tallied in the proper way. Every morning at sunrise, the president added, he would personally come to the ship to make sure that all their needs were taken care of and that they were happy with the process.

The following morning at sunrise, the president went to the ship. To his amazement, the sealed box was on deck, and Akhbar Hona, standing next to it, told the president that every animal had already voted. The box was taken back to the grand meeting room of the General Assembly, where the ambassadors had been hastily gathered. When everybody had been seated, the president said: "Ladies and gentlemen, the box is full, and the animals have made their choice. Ambassador Hona and myself will now proceed with the counting of the ballots. The species that has received the highest number of votes will be the one selected, and it will be the mandatory duty of this assembly to see that the will expressed by this vote is carried out, which will unfortunately lead to the sad but mandatory extinction of an animal species from this planet."

Under the watchful eyes of the assembly, the president unsealed the box. One at a time, he removed the ballots, reading and handing them to Ambassador Hona, who stacked them in neat piles on the table under the appropriate labels. Within hours, the task had been almost completed, and there was only one ballot left in the box. The president picked it up and gave it to Hona. The ambassador looked at it and put it on the same pile as all the other ballots that had been in the box. Each and everyone of them bore the same short name. That of Man.

~~~~~

What Is a Beluga?

1. WHAT'S IN A NAME?   The word *beluga,* or as it is sometimes written, *belukha,* is the English version of the whale's Russian name, белуха, from белый, meaning white. It therefore obviously refers to a white whale. To the French people who presently live by the St. Lawrence River in Québec, it is known as *le béluga.* People in France prefer to say *le bélouga*, since of course the whale must not be mistaken for the other *béluga,* the caviar providing sturgeon, whose name is spelled белуга in Russian.

Marie-Simonne's father, who hunted belugas in the St. Lawrence in the early 1900s, gave the animal its ancient name of *marsouin.* This is in fact the French word for porpoise, but somehow it seemed appropriate to the French colonists who settled on the river from the 1600s onward. When Jacques Cartier encountered the species in 1535 in the St. Lawrence for the first time, he wrote down the whale's name as *Adothuys.* That was probably as close as his foreign ear could get to the actual Amerindian name in use at the time. The Inuit of northern Québec now call it *kilalugak* (plural *kilalugait*). There may be as many names as there are peoples! The beluga whale that, 457 years after Cartier, ended up in the *Tchornoï Muore,* that is, the *Mer Noire,* or Black Sea, was a *beyaz balina*—white whale again—to the Turks, who call the Black Sea *Kara Deniz.* What do belugas call themselves? Some trill perhaps, but certainly not *Delphinapterus leucas*, or white dolphin without a fin, its official scientific name.

2. WHERE THE BELUGA ROAMS. Belugas live in arctic and subarctic waters all around the polar seas, roaming as far north (82° N) as open waters, channels, and leads in the ice will allow them to. Although stray animals have been seen off New Jersey (39° N), the southernmost resident populations are found in the Sea of Okhotsk (50° N) off the east coast of Siberia and in the St. Lawrence estuary (48° N) in southeastern Canada.

Being circumpolar, belugas are found in the waters of Alaska, Russia, Spitzbergen, Norway, Greenland, and Canada. The total Canadian population is presently estimated at 40,000–110,000 animals. The largest concentration is that of Hudson Bay, composed of 30,000–60,000 whales. Another 20,000–40,000 are found in the Beaufort Sea, and 5,000–10,000 live in the high Arctic, East Baffin Island, and the St. Lawrence estuary. The latter two populations number only about 500 animals each, and it is believed that a population in Ungava Bay (northern Québec) has now been eliminated through overhunting.

The belugas that winter in West Greenland migrate in summer to the Canadian arctic archipelago around Somerset Island. They are joined there by others that winter in polynyas (permanent and irregular openings maintained by wind and sea currents), and together they form the Baffin Bay stock, numbering 2,000–10,000 animals. It is believed that this population has suffered a decline in the last decade. There are also smaller numbers of belugas on the east side of Greenland; these are believed to belong to populations of the European arctic and are spread around Spitzbergen, Norway, and the north coasts of Russia and Siberia, but very few data are available on their current status. There are again unknown numbers of beluga whales off the East Siberian, Chukchi, and Bering Seas and the Sea of Okhotsk in the North Pacific. Several of these formerly numerous populations may have been depleted in the last decades. On the other side of the Bering Sea, three main aggregations of at least 1,000–3,000 animals come to the coast of Alaska every summer.

In winter, beluga whales prefer medium or loose pack ice, and when found in close or compact pack ice, they concentrate in polynyas, in leads, and in fractures or cracks. They are rarely seen in open waters away from the ice. They come nearer to the coast in spring and summer, when they have the unusual habit for cetaceans of congregating in specific areas close to shore on a rather predictable schedule. It is hypothesized that individual whales may show a high fidelity to some sites, to which they return year after year. The exact features that attract animals to such sites are unknown, but migrations are thought to be driven mainly by the needs to feed, to give birth, and to rear the young. These summer aggregations occur near mouths of rivers and in estuaries, bringing animals in prolonged contact with freshwater or water of low salinity. In arctic localities, observations have shown that this contact has a physiological value related to the molting of the epidermis. Beluga whales often ascend rivers to great distances away from the sea, having been observed 500 miles up the Yukon River in Alaska, and, historically, 350 miles up the St. Lawrence River from the gulf.

3. ANATOMY OF A BELUGA WHALE.   As whales go, belugas are on the small side. The maximum recorded weight of adult males in the St. Lawrence is around three thousand pounds, for a length of fifteen feet. The heaviest females reach only 1,900 pounds and thirteen feet nine inches. Neonates weigh around 110

pounds and, at only five feet long, are about the size of a harbor porpoise, the smallest of all cetaceans. In comparison, the record blue whale, the largest animal that ever lived on earth, is said to have reached 108 feet in length, with a body weight of 196 tons.

Adult belugas are easily distinguished from all other species by their pure white skin, their size, and their lack of a dorsal fin. Neonates and very young animals are beige-brown to dark brown or gray-brown to dark gray. They can be mistaken by nonspecialists for small dolphins and porpoises, although the latter have dorsal fins, or they can be confused with narwhal newborns, which are slate gray. Juvenile belugas, which are various shades of a uniform gray color, are readily disinguished from narwhals, which are mottled and have patches of white about the anus and the genital slit. Belugas become progressively whiter after age five or six; almost all have become pure white by age ten.

The *body* appears massive and ungainly, with a broad and rounded head. The bulk of the *head* is taken up by the forehead, called the melon; the muzzle is rather flat over thick lips, without much of a rostrum, especially in older adults. Unlike other cetaceans, but sharing this trait with the narwhal and the river dolphin, belugas' cervical vertebrae are not fused. Therefore, the beluga can move its head in all directions, and when it does, a constriction around the nape of the neck becomes apparent. There is no dorsal fin, but a thickened ridge, often grayish and irregularly nicked from encounters with ice and other hard surfaces, runs down the middle of the back. The flippers are broad, paddlelike, and supported by very short but noticeable limbs; their tips curve up progressively with age in males. The tail flukes are broad and notched.

As in other cetaceans, the skin has no sweat or other glands and no hair. The epidermis is a five-to-twelve-millimeters thick layer of rubbery fat, overlaid by a filmlike, transparent row of cells that peels off easily when dry. The underlying dermis is well developed and was formerly tanned to obtain a very fine and grainless leather. Its basal layer is quite resistant and serves as a boundary with the hypodermis, or *blubber*. The thickness of this almost fiberless coat of fat can vary within an individual from four to twenty-seven centimeters, being thickest above the forehead and thinnest around the tail stock. This extensive derm (skin and blubber) accounts for 40 percent to 50 percent of the total weight of the animal.

Although males tend to have bulkier heads and broader scapular girdles (shoulders) than females, sexes cannot be readily told apart in the field. The *sex organs* are internal and the only reliable sexual characteristic is the genital slit, which is very rarely visible in the wild. In males, it is situated a few inches in front of the smaller anal opening. In females, the anal and vaginal openings are set very close to each other near the ventral base of the tail stock. The *mammary glands* are internal, but the mammae protrude on either side of the genital slit. Beluga *milk* generally contains 27 percent fat (a maximum of 52 percent has been recorded in a St. Lawrence female), 59 percent water, 11 percent protein, and 1 percent lactose, proportions not unlike those of other aquatic mammals.

As in many dolphins, the *skull* of the beluga is slightly asymmetric and elongate due to the extended rostrum, which is overlain by the melon. There are 49–54 *vertebrae* (7 cervical, 11–12 thoracic, 6–12 lumbar, 21–26 caudal). The ribs are fused ventrally to a broad sternum, giving rigidity to the cage and allowing live stranded animals to not suffocate under their own weight. Belugas have no pelvis and no hind limbs, although two very small free bones serve as sites of attachment for muscles of the urogenital system. The front limbs, commonly called *flippers*, have the same bones as the forelimbs of humans. Those of the arm (humerus, radius, and ulna) are, however, so short and squat that the shoulder is buried under the blubber, and the elbow lies close to the body. Within the broad and flat flipper lie the bones of the wrist, hand, and elongated digits.

There is a single crescent-shaped *blowhole* on the top of the head. The larynx (without vocal chords) leads to a noncollapsible trachea made of cartilagenous rings. Progressively smaller rings are present around the bronchi, bronchia, and bronchioles and prevent the collapse of the air passages to the lung alveoli under pressure at depth. The elongate lungs are single lobed.

The *heart* of the beluga whale can weigh up to twelve pounds and is characterized by transverse broadness, flatness of the ventricles from one surface to the other, and apical roundness formed by both ventricles. The aorta has a thick wall and forms an enlargement proximal to the pulmonary trunk. As in other cetaceans, the right atrium is quite a bit larger than the left. The morphology of the heart—the relatively long and very narrow right chamber, the marked sinuosity of both coronary arteries and of their main branches, the numerous large anastomoses between the major vessels, and the duplication of vessels in parallel branches—is indicative of a deep diver. A wild beluga fitted with a satellite transmitter was recorded diving to more than 2,600 feet, or about half a mile. Trained belugas have dived readily for fifteen minutes to a depth of 1,325 feet; a maximum dive of 6,500 feet has been attained, for a total distance of two and one-half miles underwater.

The mouth holds 26–40 nonspecialized, peglike *teeth* that erupt in the second year and may grow throughout life. They are thinner and shorter in females than in males, where they attain a maximum length of eight centimeters, and are worn down considerably in aged animals from abrasion against opposing teeth. The teeth are made of external layers of cementum around a central core of dentine. The latter is deposited throughout life in concentric layers, forming cones that become progressively flattened with age. Animals are aged by reading longitudinal tooth sections for groups of layers of cementum or of dentine, which are separated by darker seasonal bands indicating slower growth. Tooth wear and cessation of growth may bias the determination of age in older animals. Maximum recorded longevity in the St. Lawrence is thirty-three-plus years.

Prey are believed not to be masticated but swallowed whole. The *stomach* is three-chambered, the first and largest compartment being nonglandular, with an extensively folded, white, keratinized mucosa like that of a cow. The first section of intestine is enlarged and thickened and has sometimes been referred to as a fourth stomacal compartment. The seventy-plus-foot-long intestine is not clearly differentiated into various sections, and there is no cecum.

The kidneys are oblong and lobated. The male *testes* are oval, relatively large, each weighing up to two pounds, and are situated internally. The penis is usually pulled back in an S-shaped position inside the body by retractor muscles; even the tip is concealed inside the genital slit. Relaxation of these muscles results in the penis' extrusion, as is sometimes observed after death in large whales, although not in belugas. In females, two functional *ovaries* are present and the uterus has two horns. The single fetus is usually implanted in the left uterine horn, although full-size fetuses are often held in a bent position, with head and torso in one horn and flukes and tail stock in the other.

The beluga whale has a large *brain*, weighing up to more than 5.5 pounds, including the cerebellum. It is very similar to the human brain in overall appearance. Both the cerebellum and the cortex of the brain are quite developed. There are no olfactory structures, and the sense of hearing used for sound production and interpretation appears to be the most developed. Belugas have directional capabilities and exceptional acoustic abilities, allowing them to discriminate objects in terms of their sizes, shapes, structures, and textures. Sounds are generated by passage and vibration of air in nasal diverticula around the blowhole and larynx. They may be transmitted and amplified through the bones of the skull, rostrum, and mandible, and the connective tissue of the melon. The melon in the beluga is highly mobile, and its shape can be varied to facilitate the transmission or the reception of sounds.

4. BEHAVING LIKE A BELUGA.   When traveling in a directive manner in open water, the beluga surfaces smoothly in a slow roll every ten to fifteen seconds to respire, but less often when slow paced. Neonates have a tendency to break the surface more vertically, almost with a jump, bobbing like novice swimmers. Most observations of beluga whales describe them as slower swimmers than dolphins; they attain maximum speeds of only ten to fourteen miles per hour. They do not often breach like other whales, do not normally porpoise out of the water like dolphins, and rarely show their flukes when diving. They can submerge for relatively long periods, as is required for commonly traveling under the ice. They are capable of submerging for fifteen to thirty minutes and can cover up to 2.5 miles on one dive. They are equally at ease in shallows, easily maneuvering and somersaulting in less than six feet of water. Unlike several other species and in spite of their close association with the shore, belugas are not known to die in live strandings. Individuals in inshore bays of the Arctic are sometimes left high and dry by the receding tide, but they swim out unscathed with the flow.

Belugas are highly gregarious and are therefore presumed to have a complex social structure with appropriate and specific communication patterns and behaviors. Very little is known, however, about their social behavior, particularly in winter. Summer aggregations are thought to be differentiated into herds of males and herds of females with young, which occupy slightly different areas. Within herds, there may be smaller groups of individuals that remain closely associated for extended periods and over many years, and which may be family units representing more than one generation, as has been observed in other species. Individuals within such groups have been observed to interact with each other, for example, in supportive behavior toward a calving female, as well as with individuals of other groups upon meeting. Beluga whales, and particularly juveniles, show much curiosity toward boats and unfamiliar objects in their environment. In captivity, they are rather docile animals and can be trained easily to perform a number of tricks and tasks.

The bond between mother and neonate is strong. Calves stay close to their mothers and have been seen riding their backs. Adults have been observed carrying objects, perhaps as surrogates for lost calves. Juveniles may remain closely associated with their mothers after weaning and until they attain sexual maturity and change color, although very few factual data on this are available.

Beluga whales produce a wide variety of sounds much of the time, although they tend to be silent when traveling in a directive way. Their remarkable acoustic capability is undoubtedly particularly well adapted to a winter environment of varying ice conditions and a summer estuarine habitat of silty waters and changing channels of varying depths.

Like other toothed whales, belugas use two main functional categories of underwater sounds. The first are sounds used for communication between individuals, which are either whistles or pulsed tones; the others are clicks used for echolocation. In acoustical terms, these sounds are regrouped into pure tones (whistles), which are unpulsed sounds, and pulsed sounds (clicks and pulsed tones). Clicks are emitted in regular trains at various repetition rates and usually cover a broadband frequency spectrum that can extend into the ultrasound range (above twenty kilohertz). They are used by whales for echolocating when investigating objects in their environment, for navigating, and for finding prey and food items. Pulsed tones are more restricted in frequency range than clicks. They are emitted in rapid bursts at very high repetition and are restricted to the sonic range (below twenty kilohertz). To the human ear, they may sound like cracks, barks, squawks, or moans. Whistles are pure tones and continuous sounds within a narrowband frequency limited to the sonic range, and they may vary in pitch.

Belugas are the most vocal of odontocete cetaceans, and their repertoire is more varied than that of dolphins. Belugas are believed to surpass dolphins in terms of both their echolocation capability and their potential for social communication. However, as in other species, a relationship between a specific sound and a specific behavioral context has not been shown yet.

5. LIVING AND DYING LIKE A BELUGA. Mating has never been observed in belugas, but it is thought to occur in the spring and would therefore usually be carried out in icy waters. Delayed implantation has been hypothesized but not confirmed. As in other species of toothed whales, males probably copulate with many females, and there is probably a considerable amount of sexual activity during the mating season. Although such activity may be reduced in summer, when herds appear to be segregated into male groups and female with young pods, sexual play has been

observed twice in the St. Lawrence. In one instance, in September, five to six adults believed to be males swam around a single female close to the research boat. As with humpback whales off Hawaii, there was much excitement around the female, her suitors reacting in unison to her every move, with heads, flukes, pectoral fins, and sometimes most of their bodies flashing above water. Repeatedly, males were seen with erections. At one point, one male swam near the surface against the female, both of them upside down and half turned toward each other, the erect penis of the male touching the female a few inches from her genital slit. In the other case, in June, a pod of fifteen to twenty belugas were followed as they sped toward a smaller group in the distance. Again, this group contained a female surrounded by four to five males, and at least one animal's fully erect penis was seen several times above water.

Gestation lasts fourteen to fifteen months, and the female beluga gives birth to a single young between May and September, with a peak in July. Lactation lasts for more than one year, although solid food is also taken after the first year. This schedule calls for a reproductive cycle of three years. Females reach sexual maturity at age five or six and reproduce until the end of life, although less frequently after age twenty-one. Therefore, a single female would not have more than eight or nine offspring in her lifetime. Males reach sexual maturity between seven and nine years of age. The social breeding system is unknown.

Belugas have a varied diet of fish and invertebrates of different sizes. They feed opportunistically, taking whatever seems to be most available at a given time and place. Their food requirements are estimated to be on the order of ten to fifteen kilograms per day. This ration is no doubt easily obtained in spring and fall when fish are migrating along the coast and into estuaries, where belugas feed predominantly on species such as herring, capelin, smelt, and salmon. Belugas in the Bering Sea in winter probably feed on offshore groundfish like pollock, while migrating animals feed on shrimp, cod, squid, and octopus.

Natural predators of belugas in arctic waters are killer whales, polar bears, and people of the North. Beluga whales react strongly to killer whale sounds and will hug the coast to stay clear of them. Polar bears catch belugas in ice-covered waters, grasping them in openings in the ice where the whales come to breathe or when the whales are left stranded at low tide. Another natural cause of death is ice entrapment, in which many individuals may be frozen to death or become exhausted while congregating in a single opening surrounded by extensive ice cover. The only known life-threatening diseases in the Arctic are parasitic and viral in origin, but their rates of incidence are unknown.

Death rates and life expectancy at birth are known only from a hunted population in Alaska and from the St. Lawrence estuary population. Both are believed to be stable and suggest that the natural potential rate of increase among beluga populations is on the order of 2 to 3 percent per year. This would suggest that recovery of depleted populations can only be slow.

6. MEN AND BELUGAS. The inclination of white whales to congregate close to shore at predictable times and places has attracted man to this species. It was after seeing hunters harpoon a whale at one such location in the estuary of the Ob River in Siberia that the naturalist Peter Simon Pallas first described the species in 1776. This was obviously long after aboriginal people of the North had been hunting the whale for food and the use of its skin. Thule Eskimos hunted belugas with kayak, harpoon, and floats, a traditional technique still in use only in the Avnnaarsua

(Qaanaaq) region of northwest Greenland. Other subsistence hunters in North America and elsewhere now use high-powered rifles, motorboats, and snowmobiles to pursue their prey.

The beluga has not been immune to European intensive hunts for all kinds of sea mammals from the eighteenth to the middle of the present century. White whales were caught by Russian and Norwegian whalers from fleets using seine nets in the Arctic Ocean; they were snared in gill nets and trap nets in Siberian estuaries and in Hudson Bay; they were trapped in weirs on tidal flats and shot from boats in the St. Lawrence estuary. Most commercial hunting ceased in the 1950s, but some populations had been overexploited to the extent that they can no longer support subsistence hunting, and they are in need of protection. Currently in Canada, the St. Lawrence, Ungava Bay, and Cumberland (Southeast Baffin) populations are considered endangered, while the eastern Hudson Bay population is classified as threatened. The status of most Russian stocks is unknown.

The useful products of the whale are fat, skin, and meat. The fat from various parts of the body has been used for greasing and waterproofing and for making soap, margarine, ointments, and high-quality lubricants for precision instruments. The high quality of the beluga skin has been recognized since the eleventh century. Its leather is soft, grainless, delicate yet strong; and it has been put to many uses, including the manufacture of footwear, harnesses, soles, driving belts, and boot laces. The meat has been used for human and animal consumption as well as for fertilizer. There are no large-scale commercial hunts anywhere now, and the main value of beluga to traditional hunters in the Canadian Arctic is the consumption of its epidermis, called *maktak*, as a delicacy.

Sailors have known the white whale for a long time, having been enchanted by its remarkable voice and loquacity. The whale was known as the sea canary, and its sounds could be heard both above water and as vibrations through the hull of ships. Probably on account of this interest as well as the ease with which it could be caught near shore, the beluga whale was one of the first cetaceans kept in captivity. The first white whales displayed live seem to have been those at Barnum's Museum in New York in the early 1860s. The animals had been caught in the St. Lawrence, sent to Montréal onboard a sloop, and moved from there by railway to New York.

Belugas are still highly valuable as major attractions in aquaria. They are transported into captivity on specially commissioned planes at great cost. There are presently around fifty recorded belugas in captivity worldwide. Most originate from the same population that visits the estuary of the Churchill River in Hudson Bay, Canada. Forty of them are held in a number of North American facilities, where conditions are much improved since the days of Mr. Barnum, and some have recently reproduced successfully. The other captive belugas from Hudson Bay are held in Europe (two) and Japan (one). A small number of beluga whales from Alaska and the Sea of Okhotsk are held in Japan, the United States, and Russia. In the latter two countries, belugas have been held for many years in military facilities for studies on sonar technology, diving physiology, and other undisclosed purposes.

7. THE BELUGA AND THE ST. LAWRENCE. The presence of belugas in the St. Lawrence dates back to the end of the last glaciation, the Wisconsinian, between 12,400 and 9,300 years ago. At the height of the last ice age, around twenty thousand years ago, belugas lived in the Atlantic, feeding at the ice edge off the exposed continental shelf. Then, as the climate warmed up,

the Laurentian ice sheet melted away and the sea level rose. Since the continent had sunk considerably under the immense weight of ice, marine waters invaded far inland. In the northeast, penetrating into the Gulf of St. Lawrence, the sea filled a huge area west almost to the Great Lakes and southwest to New York and Vermont. The region was then the edge of the Arctic, and beluga fossils have been unearthed at various sites in the sediments deposited at the bottom of this inland waterway, known as the Champlain Sea.

The Gulf of St. Lawrence and the lower estuary of the St. Lawrence River have retained to this day some characteristics of glacial climates, and in some ways form an arctic oasis. In addition to the belugas, there can be found bearded seals, ringed seals, arctic cod, and a few species of crustaceans and molluscs that are typical of more northern waters. Winters are cold and prolonged, and water cooled at the surface sinks to maintain a frigid layer at intermediate depth, which in the deeper channels overlays the cold water masses continuous with those of the North Atlantic. In winter, the extensive surface ice cover gives the region the typical appearance of subarctic seas and provides extensive pupping sites for thousands of harp and hooded seals.

The deep cold waters surge year-round to the surface in several locations, bringing up to the sun the minerals that favor the growth of algal plankton. These tiny plant organisms are consumed by swarms of zooplankton that support the production of fish and that are in turn consumed by marine mammals. In addition to four species of seals, ten species of cetaceans use the area regularly, from the gigantic blue whale to the tiny harbor porpoise. The heart of the beluga range in summer is centered around a major upwelling area near the mouth of the Saguenay River and fjord.

This area is ambiguously situated between lake and sea, fresh and saline waters, continent and ocean. Technically, the St.

Lawrence River proper originates at the mouth of Lake Ontario and ends some fifty miles east of Montréal, where its delta opens onto the freshwater Lac St.-Pierre. Beyond is the St. Lawrence estuary, which flows first through a plain, then over a fault betwen two major mountain plateaus that squeeze it on either side, and finally merges with the Gulf of St. Lawrence. The gulf is a wide extension of the Atlantic Ocean that contributes a deep upstream flow to counterbalance the downstream movement of freshwater from the river. Thus, salt is still measurable two hundred miles upstream from the gulf, and tides are noticeable all the way up to Lac St.-Pierre. As the crow flies, the estuary stretches for more than three hundred miles, longer than the river itself.

Historically, in summer, belugas were seen in freshwater up to Lac St.-Pierre, and large herds roamed far to the east into the marine waters along the lower north shore of the gulf. Their present summer distribution is limited to the central portion of that range, because either the population is smaller or some preferred habitats have been lost through development. From April to October, the whales congregate in the St. Lawrence estuary on either side of the Saguenay mouth, roughly between the Bic Islands (near Rimouski) and Île-aux-Coudres, over a distance of about one hundred miles. The estuary there is nine to twenty miles wide, and troughs to depths of 975 feet are interspersed with a number of islands and reefs whose extensive shallows, swift tidal currents, and changing meteorological conditions make navigation hazardous. For the most part, the north shore is steep and rocky, while the south shore slopes down gently, exposing at low tide extensive flats of clay deposited at the bottom of the ancient Champlain Sea.

Female belugas and their young prefer the upstream half (called the middle estuary) of the range, where the life of the river is regulated by high-amplitude tides and the opposite flows of fresh and salt waters. Larger aggregations of up to two hundred-plus animals, mostly adults and possibly a majority of males, can sometimes be found in the lower half of the range (called the lower or maritime estuary), where more typical marine conditions are found. Small groups of whales of both sexes regularly ascend the Saguenay fjord for up to sixty miles inland into freshwater. In winter, the entire beluga population retreats into the looser pack ice regions of the lower estuary and gulf. There are no significant exchanges with beluga populations living in the Arctic, and the St. Lawrence beluga is essentially isolated.

The remains of butchered beluga skeletons have been unearthed at archaeological sites inhabited by Amerindians of the St. Lawrence Iroquoian tribes on Green Island across the mouth of the Saguenay, and dated at A.D. 200. At the time of his second voyage in 1535, Jacques Cartier noted the abundance of belugas and mentioned a great fishery of these whales carried out at Île-aux-Coudres by the Amerindians, who considered the whale good to eat. Basque whalers came to the St. Lawrence from France and Spain in the late 1500s to hunt right whales and may have also hunted belugas. After the founding of the colony of New France in the early 1600s, the first concessions for white whale hunting were made during the 1660s and 1670s. During the next century, entrapment technology evolved from the use of fishing nets and lines to that of poles or stakes forming extensive weirs on tidal flats, mostly on the south shore of the river. Some of these weirs were used until the mid-twentieth century almost without interruption. Starting in the nineteenth century, beluga whales were also killed with harpoons and guns, first by rather daring hunters using canoe and sail, and later the faster motorboat.

The fishery was probably quite productive right from the beginning, although there are few data on actual catches before 1866. In the late 1880s and again in the 1920s there seem to have been increases, perceived or real, in the number of whales in the St. Lawrence, when fishermen complained that the lack of fish was due to the voracity of the beluga. From 1928 until 1939, a government-sponsored program was aimed at reducing or even eradicating the beluga from the St. Lawrence. After a short and futile episode of bombing from the air, whales were landed by hunters who shot them from boats for a bounty. There was still a fishery after the Second World War, but it has not been well documented. During that time, a number of kills were also made by sports fishermen. The last weir fishery was active but not very productive from 1962 through 1970. The St. Lawrence beluga population was given a protected status in 1979.

Data from fisheries' statistics and officers' reports and from Hudson Bay Company post journals on captures and sales of hides and barrels of oil account for an average of two hundred whales killed every year in the St. Lawrence from 1866 to 1945. Using these numbers and based on the natural birth rate for the species, it is estimated that the white whale population in the St. Lawrence must have been 5,000–10,000 strong early in this century. It now numbers only about five hundred animals. Because little information exists on kills after the Second World War and no valid surveys were carried out until the 1980s, it has not been possible to document this drastic reduction in abundance and to identify its origin.

One cause may have been overhunting, culminating in the eradication effort of 1928–1939. However, following a three-year lull, there were still large numbers of whales during the war, with a catch again of over two hundred whales per year in 1942–44. There was apparently no drastic decline in yield from 1945 through 1953, although the documented kills were definitely fewer than earlier. This may indicate a smaller population, but it cannot be ruled out that there were actually more kills, although undocumented, or that there was little hunting effort for lack of a market for whale products.

Habitat degradation or destruction is another possible cause of the decline. After the war, there was extensive harbor building, dredging, and lock construction for the seaway, as well as hydro-electric development along the St. Lawrence and Great Lakes. These may have led to decreases in water quality and fish pro-ductivity as well as to habitat loss. In support of this hypothesis, it has often been observed that large herds of belugas are no longer found at the mouth of the Manicouagan River (across from Rimouski), where a large hydroelectric complex was built during the 1960s. Noise pollution and interference by boats are other forms of habitat degradation that have increased in recent years due to whalewatching and tourism centered on a national marine park in the heart of the beluga range.

A fourth hypothesis is that the increasing flow of toxic chem-icals in the Great Lakes and St. Lawrence ecosystems after the war has been detrimental to the health of the beluga population, in terms of both increased mortality and reduced fertility. A study initiated in 1982 has shown high levels of nonbiodegradable organochlorines, lead, and mercury, as well as evidence of expo-sure to carcinogenic hydrocarbons in the whales' tissues, all orig-inating from the local and migrating fish and invertebrates on which the whales feed. Some of these toxic chemicals are passed on to calves through their mothers' milk. During their first year of life, the calves' diet is composed almost exclusively of milk, which is much more contaminated than the fish eaten by their own mothers. In ecological terms, this means that relative to adults, calves feed at a higher level in the food chain, where toxic chemicals have been further bioconcentrated.

Soon after their introduction to North America in the 1930s and 1940s, the more ubiquitous organochlorines started to accumulate in belugas, as evidenced by a sample of blubber oil from the early 1950s, which contained eight parts per million of PCBs and twenty-nine parts per million of DDT. Because of transfer through milk, each new generation of calves started its free-feeding life with a blubber organochlorine level above that of their mothers. In turn, they took fish from a system that was receiving more chemicals every year, which led to an escalation, each generation starting from a less advantageous position than the previous one. Today, the burdens of toxic chemicals in adult females are still high, in spite of drastic decreases in the levels observed in fish and invertebrates of the St. Lawrence–Great Lakes system.

Autopsies on beluga carcasses found on shore or adrift have shown a high incidence of various types of chronic health problems that are often multiple and that affect several organs. Some are suggestive of immunosuppression, and, along with evidence of reproductive impairment, endocrine dysfunction, and gastric ulcers, are consistent with the effects of organochlorines observed in other animals. Many of the above, as well as other acute lesions in St. Lawrence belugas (such as perforated gastric ulcers and aneurysms of the pulmonary trunk) had not been reported previously in cetaceans. In addition, and perhaps most striking, the St. Lawrence beluga has by far the highest incidence of cancer of any marine mammal, in fact higher than that found in man and domestic animals (except dogs). The most common cancer observed in belugas—an epithelial cancer of the small intestine—is exceeded only among sheep in pastures treated with herbicides in certain parts of the world.

It is likely that a combination of overhunting, habitat reduction or degradation, and toxic chemical exposure has led the population to its present low level. It has been suggested that this small size may have led to inbreeding and resulted in the sharing of deleterious traits, such as infertility or a greater susceptibility to the effects of exposure to toxic chemicals. Some preliminary genetic studies indeed suggest that the St. Lawrence population is distinct from those in the Arctic and that its members share some traits more commonly than do those that live elsewhere. However, the St. Lawrence beluga is also closely related to the large population living in Hudson Bay, with which it may have been in regular contact in the past. The high numbers of whales killed in the St. Lawrence in 1942–44 indicate that the local population was still quite large only fifty or so years ago. There may therefore have been little opportunity for significant genetic differentiation to occur in such a short period of time in this long-lived animal species with a low reproductive rate.

That the population has failed to increase since its protection in 1979 is a cause for worry and indicates that one or more of the above deleterious factors are still active. Autopsies suggest that chemical pollution is a major culprit, for the levels of toxic chemicals in the whales are above those known to cause health and reproductive effects in laboratory animals. Since 1982, there has been no improvement in the health condition of the St. Lawrence beluga whales. Only the future will tell if the population can still be saved.

INDEX